LOST RAILWAYS
OF
EAST ANGLIA

CW00552449

Leslie Oppitz

COUNTRYSIDE BOOKS
NEWBURY, BERKSHIRE

First published 1999
© Leslie Oppitz 1999
Reprinted 2000, 2003, 2005, 2009, 2012, 2016, 2019

COUNTRYSIDE BOOKS
3 Catherine Road
Newbury, Berkshire

To view our complete range of books,
please visit us at
www.countrysidebooks.co.uk

ISBN 978 1 85306 595 8

The cover picture shows a Class 4MT 2-6-0 locomotive standing
alongside BR Standard Class 7 Pacific locomotive No. 70013
Oliver Cromwell at Norwich station in the 1960s.
(From an original painting by Colin Doggett)

Produced through The Letterworks Ltd., Reading
Printed in Poland

CONTENTS

ABBREVIATIONS

The following abbreviations are used on numerous occasions in this book:

BR	British Rail
BVR	Bure Valley Railway
CVRPS	Colne Valley Railway Preservation Society
E&MR	Eastern & Midland Railway
EARM	East Anglia Railway Museum
ECR	Eastern Counties Railway
ESR	East Suffolk Railway
EUR	Eastern Union Railway
EW&S	English Welsh & Scottish Railway
GER	Great Eastern Railway
GNR	Great Northern Railway
GWR	Great Western Railway
K&T	Kelvedon, Tiptree & Tollesbury Pier Light Railway
LMS	London, Midland & Scottish Railway
LNER	London & North Eastern Railway
LT&S	London, Tilbury & Southend Railway
M&GN	Midland & Great Northern Joint Committee
MNR	Mid-Norfolk Railway
MR	Midland Railway
MSLR	Mid-Suffolk Light Railway
N&ER	Northern & Eastern Railway
NNR	North Norfolk Railway
T&W	Thetford & Watton Railway
W&B	Wivenhoe & Brightlingsea Railway
W&WLR	Wells & Walsingham Light Railway
WVR	Waveney Valley Railway

ACKNOWLEDGEMENTS

Acknowledgements are due to the many libraries and record offices throughout East Anglia who have delved into records, and to the late J. L. Smith of Lens of Sutton and John H. Meredith for their help in the supply of many early pictures.

Thanks also go to the following who contributed with information:

Mike Stanbury, Vice Chairman of Trustees, The East Anglian Railway Museum; Lt Cmdr R. W. Francis of the Wells & Walsingham Light Railway; Roger Gregory of the Mid-Suffolk Light Railway Museum; John Hull and members of the Mid Norfolk Railway Preservation Trust; W. D. Armstrong, Company Secretary, the Bure Valley Railway; Jonathan Wheeler, Collections Manager at the Bressingham Live Steam Museum; J. R. Hymas, The Colne Valley Railway; John Durrant, Secretary of the Midland and Great Northern Joint Railway Society.

Personal thanks go to the following for their help: Geoff Allen, Stoke Ferry; Mrs Gloria Abbott, Bury St Edmunds; John M. Cooper; 'Bob' Jenkins, Fransham; Dr Eric Savory; Chris and Judith Smith, Moulton; D. S. Williams; Brian Butler for preparing the maps. Finally, thanks go to my ailing Amstrad PCW which only just made it, Gareth Watkin of Abbeycolor, Oswestry, for helping with photographic reproduction and, as ever, thanks to my wife Joan for her patience and assistance.

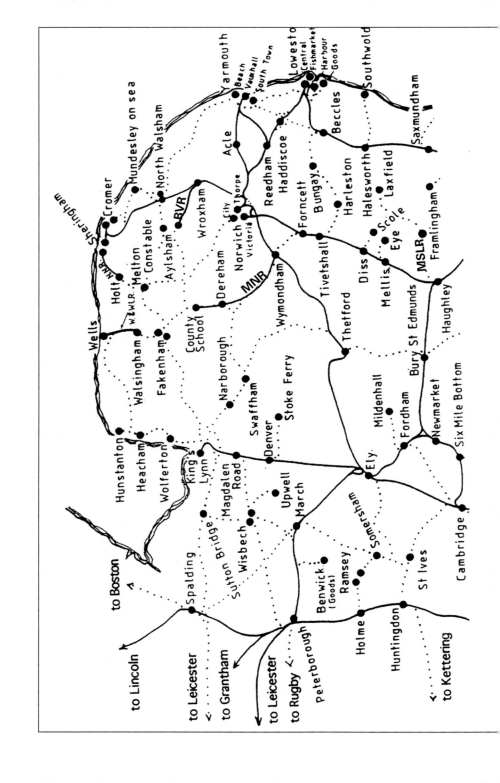

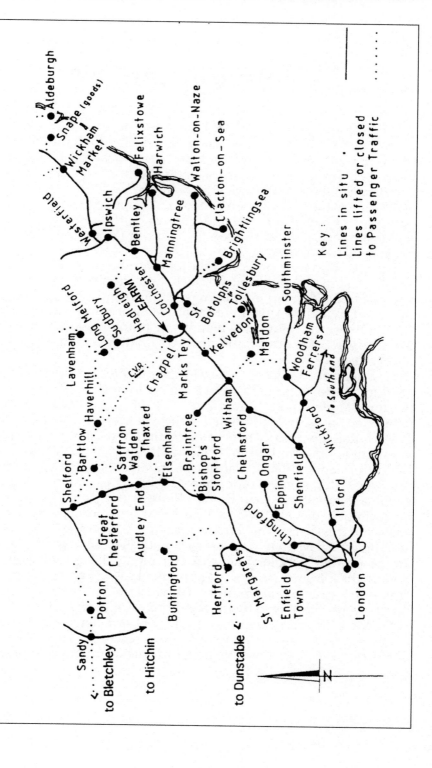

Introduction

A steam train hauled by 'Black Five' 4-6-0 locomotive no 44767 LMS class 5MT *George Stephenson* pulls into Sheringham station. Soon the platform is crowded as many passengers alight, excited children pulling parents along behind them. This scene could have taken place during any summer month in the early 1900s when the railways enjoyed great popularity. Yet it was Saturday, 24th October 1998 and a North Norfolk Railway train had just pulled in from Holt on the restored Poppy Line during a weekend half-term run.

The above scene typified earlier times throughout many East Anglia resorts. Today many branch lines in the region have disappeared. Old station buildings, engine sheds, road bridges or overgrown trackbeds are all that is left of what was once a vast network of railways when steam trains made their way across open stretches of countryside, linking remote villages and towns.

First ideas for railways in East Anglia included a proposal in 1836 for a line to be built from London to York via Dunmow, Saffron Walden and Cambridge. Yet of the various plans submitted, those which gained approval were a Northern & Eastern Railway (N&ER) line from Islington to Cambridge and, at the same time, an Eastern Counties Railway (ECR) project to build from Shoreditch to Yarmouth. It was this latter company that was later to overcome many of its rivals and form the eventual basis of the Great Eastern Railway (GER).

Although the N&ER and ECR were both incorporated in 1836, progress was slow. First activity on ECR tracks came on 18th June 1839 when two trains, each with a locomotive fore and aft, proceeded parallel to each other along the 5 foot gauge double track from a temporary terminus at Mile End to another temporary structure at Romford. Guns were fired in salute and guests were entertained by the band of the Coldstream Guards.

Yet the ECR soon experienced financial problems and it was another year before Brentwood was reached. There were disputes with landowners and, to make matters worse, shareholders in Norfolk and Suffolk began proceedings to acquire the land so that construction at their end of the line could commence. By 1843, seven years after the two companies had been incorporated, the N&ER had only reached as far as Bishop's Stortford and the ECR had reached Colchester.

In 1844 there were two important events. Firstly, the ECR took over the working of the N&ER although the latter remained a separate company for many years. Secondly, both companies (showing more foresight than the GWR) changed their gauge from 5 foot to 4 foot 8½ inches, conforming with the many other railways of the day.

Meantime, the Norfolk shareholders, frustrated at the ECR's slow progress, promoted their own Yarmouth & Norwich company to build a line which opened on 1st May 1844. In order to improve communication with London, a further company, the Norwich & Brandon Railway, was formed. Both this company and the Yarmouth & Norwich were later to be united as the Norfolk Railway. Eventually on 30th July 1845, Norwich was reached from London via Cambridge when the Norfolk Railway met the ECR's route from London at Brandon.

Further lines followed. The Eastern Union Railway (EUR), also frustrated with the ECR's lack of progress, was formed, with trains soon to reach Norwich via Ipswich, but the EUR succumbed to the ECR in 1854. From 1859 the East Suffolk Railway provided a direct link between Ipswich and the towns of Lowestoft and Yarmouth, yet even this was operated by the ECR from the day it opened.

A large number of East Anglia's branch lines came about through the ECR's failure to build new lines. The company gained a reputation for poor services and bad time-keeping and it had no money for expansion. Because of this, many districts requiring railway access had to promote their own lines or come to terms with the ECR. On 1st August 1862, the ECR was incorporated into the GER.

Another major route stretching across much of the Fens and Norfolk was that of the Midland & Great Northern Joint Committee (M&GN). These lines had been formed out of a number of independent companies which eventually became the M&GN on 1st July 1893.

This book intends to examine not only the lives of these lines, their decline and closure but also covers the many preservation societies of today that are dedicated to keeping the past alive. Apart from providing the reader with a means to explore the many 'lost' stations and trackbeds that have survived, the book includes details of the numerous societies that are proving popular through East Anglia.

Leslie Oppitz

1
Great Eastern Lines From King's Lynn

King's Lynn to Hunstanton
Heacham/Wells/Fakenham
King's Lynn to Dereham
Magdalen Road to Wisbech
Wisbech and Upwell Tramway
Denver to Stoke Ferry

The King's Lynn to Hunstanton line was initially assured of success opening at a time when many holidaymakers were coming to the Norfolk coast. Hunstanton station, photographed here c1910, became a large car park after closure in 1969. (Lens of Sutton)

Hunstanton not long before closure of the line in 1969. (Lens of Sutton)

King's Lynn to Hunstanton

A steam train arrives at Wolferton station, pulling up with the main doorway of the Royal Saloon exactly opposite the double doors to the station's main hallway. A visiting foreign King and Queen alight to be greeted by King Edward VII and Queen Alexandra. The gentlemen make for King Edward's room for a drink and a smoke and the ladies go to the larger and lighter room of Queen Alexandra to take tea.

When the Royals have left the station area, the hard work begins. The accompanying servants unload the baggage and set off on the walk of over two miles to Sandringham House. The mountains of trunks and cases are then loaded onto carts by further servants and hauled up the hill to Sandringham where the bags are taken to the appropriate rooms. There the proper attire is laid out for the forthcoming formal reception.

When completed, word passes back to Wolferton station where the Royals are still entertaining their guests. Often an inspection of the troops paraded in the station drive followed, after which the Royal party proceeded by carriage to Sandringham.

Dersingham station is today a yard for building materials. The Lynn & Hunstanton Railway opened on 3rd October 1862 eventually to become absorbed by the GER in 1890. The station became unstaffed in 1966 and finally closed to passengers in May 1969. (Author)

The above scene could be witnessed many times at Wolferton station on the line from King's Lynn to Hunstanton, with the station's greatest period undoubtedly in the early 1900s during the reign of King Edward VII. Between 1884 and 1911, no fewer than 645 Royal Trains steamed into or out of this little station. Today the station stands empty and run down. But there are plans to renovate the area following purchase by the Royal Sandringham Estate although, at the time of writing this book, the station's precise future role had not yet been decided.

Trains first reached King's Lynn in 1846 and the town had not particularly welcomed them. The port authorities claimed that their sea-going trade would decline instead of expand and, when a through line to London became available, their deliberations proved correct with the majority of goods carried direct to the capital by rail. The line from King's Lynn to Hunstanton opened on 3rd October 1862. It was initially assured of success for this was a time when holidaymakers were coming to the Norfolk coast in large numbers. Hunstanton was promoted as a new resort and the many visitors by rail ensured that the line worked at a profit. The station has today gone completely – surrendered to the motor age to become the resort's large car park.

Heacham/Wells/Fakenham

Heacham station, about a mile west of the village, served as a junction where trains left the Hunstanton line for Wells on the West Norfolk Junction Railway which opened on 17th August 1866. The company lasted only eight years before it was merged with the Lynn & Hunstanton Railway. Sixteen years later in 1890 it was absorbed by the GER. The Heacham to Wells line closed to passengers in June 1952.

King's Lynn station in the 1960s. In the early 1920s over a dozen trains ran daily to Hunstanton with many going on to Wells, Dereham or Norwich Thorpe. (Lens of Sutton)

Near the former Heacham station an old signal box survived a number of years following closure but this has gone to make way for a housing estate. The abandoned line through to Wells proved interesting. Sedgeford station building remains as a private house complete with its station sign and GER notices. On the level-crossing gate a notice reads: 'Failure to shut the gate – fine 40/-'. At Wells, correctly known as Wells-next-the-Sea, the station building became known as Burnham Potteries. The owner bemoaned that the only relic of the past that remained was the Ladies Room sign. Not far from Wells station just off the A149 can be found the Wells & Walsingham Light Railway which opened in 1982 along a stretch of 10¼ inch gauge track (see chapter 5).

The Wells & Fakenham Railway opened on 1st December 1857. When it became part of the GER in 1862 it assumed greater importance, becoming part of a north-south line carrying food to London's increasing markets. The intermediate town of Walsingham had been for many centuries one of England's major religious pilgrimage centres attracting Royalty and ordinary folk alike. When the railway became available, many thousands would frequently alight from specials on occasions of major festivals to form processions to either the Anglican or Roman Catholic shrine in the different parts of the town. Often there were 'Roman Catholic Specials' which would halt about a mile short of the station nearer the shrine.

The line closed to passengers on 5th October 1964, surviving for goods traffic only until the end of the month. It was perhaps appropriate that Walsingham station should become a Russian Orthodox monastery. The station building acquired golden domes with services held in the old booking hall.

King's Lynn to Dereham

The line from King's Lynn to Dereham opened in various stages from 1846 to 1848. The Lynn & Dereham Railway became part of the East Anglian Railway in 1847 and, like the Wells & Fakenham Railway, was incorporated into the GER in 1862.

17

At Fransham on the King's Lynn to Dereham line, not only has the station building survived as a private residence but rolling stock includes a Ruston & Hornby 88DS diesel shunter and a five-compartment suburban coach built at Stratford in 1891. (Author)

Even though the promoters had great hopes for the line, the single track initially carried only three or four trains daily, rising to nine in the early 1900s. In September 1955 diesel multiple-units were introduced but, despite such economies, the line closed completely on 9th September 1968 except for a short stretch for freight from King's Lynn to Middleton.

The former intermediate station at Fransham is today a private residence. Not only does the station building and platform still exist, but rolling stock standing on short sections of track includes a Ruston & Hornsby 88DS diesel shunter, passenger coach no 1235 which started life as a five-compartment, four-wheel suburban carriage built in 1891, and an ex-LMS Horse Box body. Recent additions at Fransham include a 2 foot gauge ex-colliery Ruston & Hornsby diesel, which will shortly be running over 100 yards of track.

Magdalen Road in the 1960s, known as Watlington until 1875. The station buildings are currently fenced off. Closed in 1968, re-opened in 1975, today known once again as Watlington.(Lens of Sutton)

Magdalen Road to Wisbech

The line from Magdalen Road to Wisbech was originally part of the East Anglian Railway system, another to be incorporated into the GER in 1862. Magdalen Road, known as Watlington until 1875, became a junction in 1848 when a branch to Wisbech was completed. Intermediate stations were Middle Drove, Smeeth Road and Emneth. The line closed to passengers on 9th September 1968 but Magdalen Road station on the main Ely to King's Lynn line re-opened on 5th May 1975 following local efforts to encourage the use of trains.

Wisbech station (spelt Wisbeach until May 1877) became Wisbech East in September 1948. The town once boasted two separate stations and two harbour branches (M&GN and GER). The M&GN line closed in 1959; the Harbour North branch closed in 1965 and the Harbour East branch the following year.

When the GER station closed in 1968, a freight-only line

An ex-GCR corridor brake composite no 51681 seen at Ely on 8th June 1951. (John H. Meredith)

remained in existence from Whitemoor junction (north of March) to Wisbech goods yard for the conveyance of Spillers pet food, Metal Box products plus coal traffic. Apart from this occasional freight traffic, Wisbech has little today to remind its inhabitants of its previous railway connections. Wisbech (East) station building has survived, currently serving as a centre for children with learning difficulties.

Wisbech & Upwell Tramway

From 1883 the GER supported a further venture with the building of the seven and three quarter mile long Wisbech & Upwell Steam Tramway to assist agriculture in the area as well as provide passenger traffic. The original tram locomotives were designed by Thomas Worsdell (GER Locomotive Super-intendent 1881–1885), being 0-4-0 tanks. They had cow-catchers, warning bells and governors which shut off steam and applied brakes should 10 mph be exceeded. Between 1903 and 1921 a

The Wisbech & Upwell Tramway c1910. The original 0-4-0 tram locomotives were fitted with cow-catchers and warning bells and were enclosed in wooden casing giving more the appearance of a freight brake van. (Lens of Sutton)

number of the original locomotives were replaced by more powerful 0-6-0T fully enclosed locomotives (GER class C53) designed by Holden (GER Locomotive Superintendent 1885–1907).

During much of the tramway's life there were eight trams daily. It lasted until 1928 for passengers and after closure, one of the bogie coaches found its way to a section of disused track near Camerton in Avon where it was used for the filming in 1953 of *The Titfield Thunderbolt*.

Finally on 23rd May 1966, the last goods tram made its way along the track, accompanied by a convoy of cars. A newspaper reported that: 'The Wisbech and Upwell Tramway went out of operation quietly and even a little ignominiously'.

Denver to Stoke Ferry

There were no serious difficulties during construction of the branch to Stoke Ferry except where the ground was found to be

Passenger traffic along the branch line from Denver to Stoke Ferry which opened in August 1882 was poor throughout. Despite economies, passenger traffic came to an end in 1930 although goods survived until 1965. Stoke Ferry station is seen here c1910. (Lens of Sutton)

very boggy. Numerous culverts were necessary and in one instance time was lost filling in a pond. The construction of Stoke Ferry station provided the greatest obstacle because of marshland. It proved necessary to remove the top-soil to a depth of twelve feet and then build brick arches to support the building and platform.

Services began on 1st August 1882 with six trains daily between Stoke Ferry and Downham Market, with some going on to King's Lynn. Passenger traffic was poor and economies were soon necessary. Ticket offices along the branch were closed and conductor-guard working was introduced. Freight traffic helped to keep the line busy and the building of a sugar beet factory at Wissington in 1925 did much to increase the branch's status.

By the middle 1920s, bus competition was taking what little

The site of Stoke Ferry station in October 1998. The station building and engine shed are currently used by a timber importer. (Author)

passenger traffic remained. It came as no surprise when the branch closed to passengers on 22nd September 1930 although freight traffic was to continue for a number of years. In 1941 the Ministry of Agriculture took over the Wissington lines followed by purchase six years later. By the mid-1960s all that remained was freight traffic between Denver and the Wissington factory which was to survive some years further.

When visiting Stoke Ferry some years ago, the author found the station building and goods shed still in existence but the water tower, the crane and the signal box had gone. The station area is currently used by timber importer, Geoff Allen. While walking the area, a shout came from a nearby property. 'Ernie' Pedditt, Leading Porter at Stoke Ferry from 1942 to 1965 called, 'If you're here to catch a train, the last one went well over 60 years ago . . .'

2
Midland And Great Northern Joint Lines

Spalding/Sutton Bridge/South Lynn
Sutton Bridge/Wisbech/Peterborough
King's Lynn to Norwich and the Norfolk Coast

A steam locomotive, probably a 4-4-0 Beyer Peacock at Sutton Bridge, c1910. The station opened in July 1862 serving lines westwards beyond Spalding. By 1865 trains reached South Lynn and in the following year a line reached Peterborough via Wisbech. (Lens of Sutton)

By the time the Eastern Counties Railway (ECR) reached King's Lynn in 1848 and Wells-next-the-Sea in 1849, the company was in truculent mood. It claimed that its network left 'not a single opening for any rival line'. However, circumstances were to prove otherwise, although it took many years for the rival Midland & Great Northern Joint Railway (M&GN) to make its presence felt.

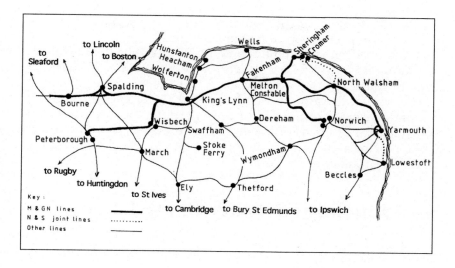

Yet not all went well for the Eastern Counties Railway. In 1860 it was claimed that its trains were no longer punctual, its fares and freight rates were excessive and accidents were far too frequent. The company's finances worsened and on 7th August 1862, the ECR became part of the newly-formed Great Eastern Railway. Meantime, rivalry continued with the Midland Railway (MR) and the Great Northern Railway (GNR) joining forces to gain access to the East Coast.

The first railway in East Anglia, which was later to become part of the M&GN in 1893, came in November 1858 when the Norwich & Spalding Railway Company completed eight miles of track from Spalding to Holbeach. Sutton Bridge was reached nearly four years later in July 1862. Earlier, on 6th August 1861, an Act had been approved granting the Lynn & Sutton Bridge Railway powers to build a line from Sutton Bridge to a junction with the ECR Ely-King's Lynn line near South Lynn. Further Acts followed. In 1862 came agreement to build from Spalding to Bourne and in July 1866 the three companies amalgamated to form the Midland & Eastern Railway.

Further gains followed in Norfolk when in January 1883 the Lynn & Fakenham Railway, the Yarmouth & North Norfolk and the Yarmouth Union amalgamated to form the Eastern &

Midlands Railway. The amalgamation also included the Peterborough, Wisbech & Sutton Bridge Railway which, until that time, had remained independent. In July 1883 the Eastern & Midlands Railway (E&MR) went on to absorb the Midland & Eastern Railway.

The Midland Railway (MR) and the GNR had throughout maintained strong interests in these various companies and it was a logical progression when on 1st July 1893, the Midland & Great Northern Joint Railway (M&GN) was formed which at the same time took over the Eastern & Midlands.

Spalding/Sutton Bridge/South Lynn

A line from Spalding to Sutton Bridge opened on 3rd July 1862 with the further section to South Lynn following nearly three years later on 1st March 1865. On 1st August 1866 a line opened westwards from Spalding to Bourne and in 1893, trains reached Little Bytham Junction, later to be officially described as the M&GN system's furthest westerly point.

When the Lynn & Sutton Bridge Railway built eastwards from Sutton Bridge, the existing 1850 cast and wrought iron Cross Keys swing-bridge designed by Robert Stephenson shared road and rail traffic, the latter crossing the river by a single track. Towards the end of the century the bridge proved inadequate and a new structure was built in 1897 slightly to the south, the change of location being the reason for the subsequent sharp curve out of Sutton Bridge station. The new bridge was operated by hydraulic power and the cost of building, £80,000, was borne by the M&GN. When the railways closed in the 1960s, the rail trackbed was turned into a road surface, now carrying westbound traffic.

Not far from Spalding can be found the former Moulton station which closed to passengers in March 1959 and to goods traffic in June 1964. After many changes it was purchased by the Smith family who, after much hard work and renovation, turned 'Station House' into a family home. Most of the up platform has gone but the old waiting room is still there – now called 'The Travellers' Rest'. Chris and Judith Smith provide a

Cross Keys bridge on the former M&GN South Lynn/Spalding line which spans the river Nene east of Sutton Bridge, today exclusively used by road traffic. The bridge, seen here in September 1988, was built in 1897 since the previous structure had proved inadequate. (Author)

Bed & Breakfast service and visitors sitting in the dining room may well care to reflect it was once the Ladies Waiting Room!

Sutton Bridge/Wisbech/Peterborough

A line southwards from Sutton Bridge via Wisbech to Peterborough opened to passengers on 1st August 1866. M&GN trains joined the Midland main line just north of Peterborough North station, crossing the main lines by Rhubarb Bridge, so called because when the embankments were built up from nearby farms, rhubarb roots continued to flourish in the earth for many years. Apart from providing a useful route for holidaymakers heading for the East Coast each summer, the line also became busy with the carriage of fruit and agricultural products.

Moulton Station between Spalding and Sutton Bridge closed to passengers in March 1959. Today the waiting room on the up line has become 'The Travellers' Rest', housing a small bar. Station House opposite provides Bed & Breakfast accommodation. (Author)

Today, some 40 years after closure of the lines to passengers, numerous intermediate stations can still be found. Many are now private dwellings although Sutton Bridge station site became an industrial area. The Wisbech M&GN station gave way to housing with 'Cricketers' Way' marking the site.

King's Lynn to Norwich and the Norfolk Coast

The Lynn & Fakenham Railway began services between King's Lynn and Melton Constable in January 1882 and by December 1882, trains reached Norwich. Services from Melton Constable to the coast at Cromer followed five years later on 16th June 1887. Initially the GER station at King's Lynn was used, leaving

Melton Constable station in earlier times. When trains arrived in 1882, the Melton Constable area developed rapidly both as a junction and a works village. (Lens of Sutton)

The bus shelter on the B1354 at Melton Constable carries reminders of earlier times. Apart from a drawing of a 4-4-2 tank locomotive, it includes two spandrels originally from the railway station. (Author)

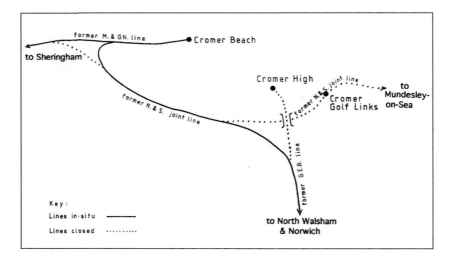

the Hunstanton branch at Gaywood Junction. When a loop line at Lynn opened in 1886, the Gaywood section was closed and trains could now travel from stations such as Sutton Bridge to Norfolk without reversal.

At the centre of what was to become the M&GN's eastern section was Melton Constable. The area developed rapidly after a railway junction had been constructed and a railway works established. To encourage labour in such an isolated place, houses were built and the railway company paid the rents. The first houses constructed in Melton Street and Astley Terrace, although of poor quality, were built for £150 each!

A number of station buildings still exist along the line eastwards from King's Lynn, via Melton Constable to Norwich. One is at Massingham where 'Station House' is today a private dwelling where a signal box remains in good condition. Fakenham West station has gone but a short section of platform edge can still be seen along the B1146 Fakenham/Dereham road by Jewson's yard.

The works buildings at Melton Constable were constructed with brick and iron and made to last, being still in existence to this day. A water tower still exists above the factory area and closer inspection shows where shrapnel holes have been

Cromer High station c1910, was opened by the East Norfolk Railway (later GER) when it completed a route from Norwich in 1877. The station closed in September 1954 and Cromer Beach (today known merely as Cromer) became the town's only station. (Lens of Sutton)

successfully 'patched up' following a German air raid during the Second World War. Another reminder of earlier times is the bus shelter near a road junction on the B1354 which incorporates two ornamental spandrels originating from Melton Constable station. Unexpectedly, the spandrels carry the initials CNR which stand for the Central Norfolk Railway – a company that never obtained an Act but was promoted to provide a link between Melton Constable and North Walsham. The line was eventually built by the Lynn & Fakenham with the co-operation of the Yarmouth & North Norfolk.

At Attlebridge, the station building, although converted, has maintained the characteristic M&GNR bargeboard pattern on part of its roofing. Norwich City closed to passengers on 2nd March 1959 but continued for freight purposes until almost ten years later. When it closed on 3rd February 1969 (the site became City Industrial Estate), the line was cut back to Lenwade where a 'One Train' single-line light railway continued for a number of years to serve a local firm specialising in prefabricated housing sections and concrete girders.

North Walsham GER station, c1910, which survives today on the Norwich/Cromer line. M&GN trains served North Walsham until 1959 on a route from Melton Constable to Yarmouth Beach. (Lens of Sutton)

Northwards from Melton Constable the line between Holt and Sheringham is currently put to good use by the North Norfolk Railway (chapter 5). In contrast to the original Sheringham station, now the North Norfolk Railway terminus, the resited Anglia Railways station across the road seemed little more than an apology. The line to Cromer (previously Cromer Beach) uses the former M&GN route. Since Cromer is a terminus, a reversal is necessary after which the DMUs use track once worked by the Norfolk & Suffolk Joint Railways Committee – a joint co-operation between the M&GN and the GER to avoid unnecessary duplication of routes. Subsequently the trains join the former GER line south of Cromer High (closed to passengers in 1954) to reach Norwich. At Cromer the station building carries the E&MR motif in its arched supports.

The most easterly point reached by the M&GN was Yarmouth Beach. The route from Melton Constable via North Walsham was opened in sections over a six year period with completion over the whole route in April 1883. By 1887 King's Lynn services included trains to Cromer, Norwich and Yarmouth and, over further Norfolk & Suffolk Joint Railways Committee tracks,

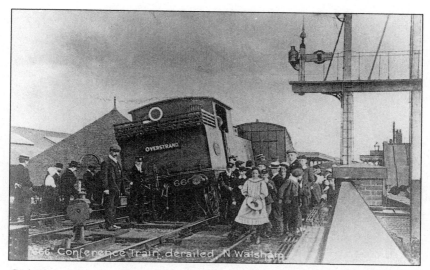

Onlookers pose for the camera after a train has derailed at North Walsham station around the turn of the 20th century. (Lens of Sutton)

trains to Mundesley and Lowestoft. In July 1906 co-operation between the M&GN and GER went further to provide a London-Sheringham service. A year later the 'Norfolk Coast Express' came into being with sections for Sheringham, Cromer High and Mundesley.

After the First World War, competition came from motorbuses and then from the private motor car. In addition many stations were a mile or so from the towns or villages they claimed to serve. Norwich City station was also some way from the city's commercial centre. It was clear that the heyday of railway monopoly was over. Despite economies, passenger and freight traffic continued to decline, although the Second World War did provide a substantial reprieve with many airfields in the area.

February 28th 1959 was a sad day for M&GN supporters when almost the entire system closed to passenger trains. Many travelled dressed in black, complete with arm bands and top hats. The locomotive hauling the last train bound for Melton Constable, 4MT no 43145, was decorated with a laurel wreath on its smokebox and a slogan read, 'Goodbye all: We may not pass

Trains reached Norwich City station, seen here in the early 1950s, from Melton Constable in 1882. After closure of Norwich City to passengers in 1959 and to goods in 1969, the station was demolished to become an industrial site. (Lens of Sutton)

this way again'. As the train left the station in a last defiant burst of steam, yards of toilet paper and coloured streamers trailed from its carriage windows.

The line between Sheringham and Melton Constable survived a further five years until closure for passengers came on 4th April 1964. Freight services continued over many lines but these were all destined for eventual failure. The writing on the rear of a brake van on the last diesel-hauled freight train from Sutton Bridge on 2nd April 1965 seemed to sum it all up. It read simply: 'That's yer lot!'

3
Yarmouth And Lowestoft

Yarmouth first saw trains when a line from Norwich via Reedham opened on 30th April 1844. By 1877 Yarmouth had three main termini, Yarmouth Vauxhall, Yarmouth Beach and Yarmouth South Town (seen here after closure). (Lens of Sutton)

Yarmouth

When a special 14-coach train first reached Yarmouth from Norwich on 30th April 1844, a local newspaper reported:

> 'The engine gave forth its note of warning, the band struck up, *See, the conquering hero comes,* the engine moved forward in its majestic might . . . the hills reverberated its warning, while the puffs of steam, heard long after its departure, sounded like the breathing of a Polypheme.'

Yarmouth South Town station entrance in the 1950s. In 1942 the station was nearly demolished when a 500 kg bomb fell on the track, luckily failing to explode. The station closed completely in 1970. (Lens of Sutton)

At the resort, after the 50 minute journey, there were celebrations in the Assembly Rooms where the dinner menu included, 'spring chickens, green geese, tongues, pickled salmon, plovers' eggs, jellies, peaches and ices'!

On the next day, public services began with seven trains each way daily. At Norwich the station site was near the subsequent Norwich Thorpe station, while the Yarmouth terminus later became Yarmouth Vauxhall (today's Yarmouth station). The opening also saw the introduction of an electric telegraph, the first in the world to be used with block signalling, although in a primitive form. It was a Cooke and Wheatstone system which at the same time could be used by members of the public to send messages, initially at 4/6d including delivery but later reduced to 2/6d.

From 1st June 1859, Yarmouth had the benefit of a second and more direct rail route to London using the East Suffolk line via Haddiscoe and Beccles. The terminus was Yarmouth South

All that remains of St Olaves station today (on the former Yarmouth/Beccles line) is this name-plate fixed to the wall of St Olaves Service Station on the main road. The station site was demolished to make way for housing. (Author)

Town sited across Breydon Water from the original (Vauxhall) station. The local newspapers were quick to praise the line for its punctuality and its spacious coaches. Trains from Ipswich divided at Beccles for Lowestoft and Yarmouth. When a curve was opened at Haddiscoe in June 1872 linking the two tracks, a service was possible between Yarmouth and Lowestoft via St Olaves.

Meanwhile, on 7th August 1877, a rival company, the Yarmouth & Stalham (Light) Railway – later to become part of the M&GN system – opened a station to be called Yarmouth Beach, to the north of Vauxhall station. By 1883 trains from Yarmouth Beach were able to reach North Walsham and Melton Constable. The way was now open for holidaymakers from the Midlands and North to reach the East Coast resort.

Almost 40 years after the first line from Norwich came into existence, a second route opened via Acle. Yarmouth was increasing in popularity with holidaymakers and also much of

Yarmouth Beach station was the M&GN's terminus for trains from North Walsham, Fakenham and South Lynn, also from Lowestoft via a loop from Norfolk & Suffolk Jt rails. Yarmouth Beach closed in 1959. (Lens of Sutton)

the steamer traffic along the coast from the river Thames was transferring to the railway. The new line, a shorter route, opened in two stages, reaching Yarmouth Vauxhall on 1st June 1883.

Yarmouth now had three stations serving different directions but two further routes were to follow. The Norfolk & Suffolk Joint Committee (a working arrangement between the GER and the M&GN) opened a line between Yarmouth Beach and South stations to Lowestoft Central on 13th July 1903, serving the numerous holiday camps and bungalow villages, Gorleston, Hopton and Corton along the route and close to the sea. The importance of this stretch of nearly 13 miles increased when the M&GN opened, also in 1903, a connecting track round the inland side of Yarmouth to cross Breydon Water by means of a swing-bridge and then over the GER route into Yarmouth Vauxhall.

During the Second World War, on 7th May 1942, Yarmouth South Town station nearly suffered a major disaster when a

500 kg bomb fell on the track, failing to explode. As luck would have it, a Naval Bomb Disposal Officer was nearby who was able to immediately defuse the bomb. In 1953, however, the station suffered badly when on 31st January the area was flooded and a signalman was trapped for 21 hours before being rescued by a boat. For a week no trains reached the station. On 21st September of the same year, the Breydon swing-bridge was closed which meant that the connection to Yarmouth Beach station was lost.

The year 1959 saw major closures around Yarmouth with the Yarmouth Beach (ex-M&GN) to North Walsham and Melton Constable line closing to all traffic and the Yarmouth South line to Haddiscoe and Beccles route (ex-GER) following. The coastal line to Lowestoft survived until 4th May 1970.

A number of relics along the old Yarmouth-Haddiscoe-Beccles line can still be found. Belton station has been lost to building development but at St Olaves, the station sign can be seen on the wall of St Olaves Service Station on the main road. The station site is today a residential area and, until a few years ago, one of the bungalows was occupied by 'Eddie' Stimpson, at one time the local station-master.

Across the river Waveney, Haddiscoe station still serves the Lowestoft-Norwich line and the earlier Haddiscoe High Level station can still be found. Perched on an embankment close to where tracks once crossed, the platforms and basic platform building were almost overgrown although to the north the signal box has been converted and extended to become a private residence. From near the signal box it is possible to look out over the river Waveney to the buttresses that once supported St Olaves swing-bridge.

Lowestoft

Much of Lowestoft's early development was due to the well known contractor Sir Samuel Peto, who owned the Norwich & Lowestoft Navigation, built the 1844 Yarmouth-Norwich line and then linked it to Lowestoft via Reedham. When rival

The 11.12 am Metro-Train DMU leaves Reedham bound for Lowestoft, September 1988. The station opened in May 1844 and in subsequent years carried a considerable trade in poultry and game. (Author)

railway systems frustrated plans for a major route westwards, Peto struck south giving Lowestoft a second route. This was the Lowestoft & Beccles Railway, which opened on 1st June 1859, leaving the town from Lowestoft Central station over a swing-bridge at Oulton Broad (originally named Carlton Colville) making for Beccles and beyond.

The port of Lowestoft expanded rapidly after coming into railway hands. In less than a century it grew to an area of 74 acres which included well over 6,000 feet of quay handling various commodities plus nearly 4,500 feet of quay linked to the fishing industry. As herring catches from the North Sea swelled the trawlers' nets, the fish were landed, sold and packed in ice for despatch by rail inland. In the early part of the 20th century, between 50,000 and 60,000 tons of fish were being landed annually, valued at over £500,000, of which the bulk left by rail for London.

Holiday traffic to Lowestoft prospered although not on the

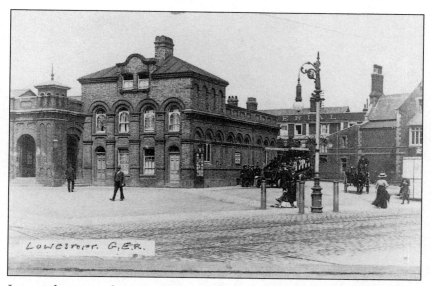

Lowestoft prospered as a seaside resort in the mid-1950s when up to 25 trains ran on Saturdays during the summer to and from Liverpool Street plus a holiday special for Gorleston. (Lens of Sutton)

scale of visitors to Yarmouth. Towards the end of the 19th century, passengers for Lowestoft on the fast trains from London changed at Beccles but by 1904 daily non-stop runs were available from Liverpool Street to both Yarmouth and Lowestoft. Traffic reached a peak in the mid-1950s when up to 25 trains in each direction ran on Saturdays during the summer.

When proposals were announced regarding closure of the East Suffolk line between Lowestoft, Beccles and Ipswich, there was considerable dismay. Lowestoft's town council chairman said that loss of the railways, 'would have very serious implications for the holiday industries and it would be serious indeed for the string of holiday camps along the coast.' A county council alderman said that closure would have an effect on the status and industrial life of the town, claiming that they were isolated enough already. The strenuous efforts to save the line were rewarded when in July 1966, the Minister of Transport, Mrs Barbara Castle, agreed that the line from Lowestoft to Ipswich should remain open.

The northern rest pier of Beccles Swing Bridge across the river Waveney on the line from Beccles to Yarmouth photographed on 19th December 1961. Trains crossed at a walking pace and until 1927 required pilotmen on the footplate. (John H. Meredith)

The signal box and power house that controlled Beccles Swing Bridge photographed in December 1961, two years after closure of the line. (John H. Meredith)

In 1970 the line from Yarmouth to Lowestoft closed but Lowestoft retained its two routes to Norwich and Ipswich. These separated at Oulton Broad North junction where the Ipswich route crossed the waterway by a swing-bridge, beyond which was once a connection to the old Kirkley goods depot.

4
GER Tracks In Mid-Norfolk

Wymondham to Fakenham
Forncett to Wymondham
Wroxham to County School

Trains first covered a line from Wymondham to Dereham when the Norfolk Railway (later absorbed by the GER) opened a branch for goods traffic on 7th December 1846 and for passengers on 15th February 1847. During the following year, a line was completed by the Lynn & Dereham Railway from Dereham via Swaffham to King's Lynn, giving Norwich trains a through cross-country route. On 20th March 1849 a further

Norwich Victoria station c1910. The terminus was once part of the original Eastern Union line to Norwich which opened in December 1849. It closed to passengers in 1916 and remained mainly for coal and cement traffic. The old buildings have long since gone. (Lens of Sutton)

Dereham station entrance in GER days c1905. The station first opened to goods in December 1846 and to passengers in February 1847 when the North Norfolk Railway opened a line from Wymondham. (Lens of Sutton)

branch connected Dereham and Fakenham and eight years later a line to the coast was completed by the Fakenham & Wells Railway.

Although the Norwich-Swaffham-King's Lynn route was kept fairly busy, the line from Dereham to Wells was never greatly used. Even when a further branch opened in 1866 linking Wells with Heacham (on the line from King's Lynn to Hunstanton) traffic remained at a low level. In 1880 passenger traffic suffered further when the rival Lynn & Fakenham Railway (later to become the M&GN) opened a line to Fakenham giving a direct route from Fakenham to King's Lynn. The Lynn & Fakenham Railway opened a separate station, Fakenham West, and there was no physical connection between the two routes.

At Fakenham East, 35 years since closure of the former Dereham/Wells line, a level-crossing gate can still be found at the end of a cul-de-sac named Fayregreen, preserved as a permanent reminder of the past. New homes cover the former station area where once existed a granary and a malting. Not far away once stood the flourishing Great Eastern Hotel.

Nothing is left of the Fakenham East station (on the Wells/Dereham line)
which closed in 1964. The area is today a housing estate. (Lens of Sutton)

Wymondham station remains active on the Peterborough to
Norwich line. It also has the honour of having been nominated
'Best Kept Station' on more than one occasion thanks to the
efforts of David Turner who has restored the down-platform
building. This houses a historic railway museum as well as a
'Brief Encounter' tea room which was opened on 8th October
1989 by *Dad's Army*'s Bill Pertwee.

Not far away is the Wymondham Abbey station newly built
by members of the Mid-Norfolk Railway Preservation Trust,
anticipating passenger services between Wymondham and
Dereham (chapter 5).

Forncett to Wymondham

On 2nd May 1881 a loop almost seven miles long was opened
between Forncett and Wymondham with one intermediate

Not far from the former Fakenham East station site can be found this level-crossing gate which has been preserved down a cul-de-sac off the old Norwich Road. (Author)

Wymondham station around the turn of the 20th century where trains from Fakenham and Dereham joined the main Norwich/Ely line. (Lens of Sutton)

Hardingham station building on the Wymondham/Dereham line, today a strictly private residence. It closed to regular passenger services in 1969. (Lens of Sutton)

station at Ashwellthorpe. This was opened by the GER and it was intended more as a relief route than for local traffic, giving through trains to North Norfolk the possibility of avoiding Norwich. The line, at one time double and of main line status, was also built partly to counter the M&GN encroachment on what the GER thought to be their 'territory'.

The line was never really successful. Had the North Norfolk coast developed to the extent the GER had hoped then it could have proved worthwhile. However, instead of the hoped-for through expresses, for a few years around 1900 only a portion of the London-Norwich train was detached at Forncett to continue on to Dereham and Wells. Perhaps the line's greatest moment was when the 'Norfolk Coast Express' was diverted via Forncett and Wymondham after floods put the Forncett-Norwich line out of action.

The loop survived until 10th September 1939 for passengers and until 4th August 1951 for goods traffic. Subsequently part of the line near Wymondham was used for the storing of

Ashwellthorpe between Forncett and Wymondham closed to passengers just after war broke out in September 1939. It has become a private residence called 'Station Bungalow'. (Author)

locomotives or carriages awaiting the scrapyard at Norwich. Ashwellthorpe station became 'Station Bungalow'.

Wroxham to County School

The branch from Wroxham to County School (on the Dereham-Fakenham line) was opened by the East Norfolk Railway in five stages from 1879 to 1882. Again there was competition from the M&GN with a line from Melton Constable to North Walsham running almost parallel to the north. At Aylsham there were rival stations known as North and South.

The GER Wroxham-County School line was designed to link east and west Norfolk and also to prevent any independent company considering a line from Norwich to Aylsham direct. Aylsham, an important market town, had not been happy at being omitted from the original East Norfolk route and was a

A branch from Wroxham to County School was opened in stages from 1879 to 1882. County School station mainly served the nearby Watts Naval Training College, a Dr Barnardo's institution from 1901 to 1954. (Lens of Sutton)

Wroxham station c1905 which opened in October 1874 when the East Norfolk Railway reached North Walsham from Norwich. The line was worked throughout by the GER. (Lens of Sutton)

50

A J. Holden 2-2-2 oil-burner locomotive no 1008 with passenger set at Worstead station between Wroxham and North Walsham. Picture probably around 1905. (Lens of Sutton)

temptation for any such speculative promoter. Trains reached Aylsham from Wroxham on 1st January 1880 but the line's value depreciated only three years later when the Eastern & Midlands (later M&GN) reached Aylsham (North).

There were initially up to nine trains each way daily on the GER line but within a few years this fell to six. The line was hardly a success although freight traffic was occasionally heavy with cattle and later beet from intermediate stations at Cawston and Reepham. During the Second World War the branch assisted with traffic to RAF Coltishall.

The Wroxham-County School line survived until 15th September 1952 when it closed to passenger traffic. On that day Aylsham station was decorated in black and white paper and Chopin's Funeral March was played. Stretches of the line remained open for freight until 1955 despite removal of the track between Reepham and Foulsham. When the M&GN system closed in 1959, Themelthorpe Curve was built to join the M&GN

and GER (later to become LNER) tracks to accommodate traffic from a concrete works at Lenwade which made prefabricated buildings, so trains could avoid a long detour. This traffic ceased in 1982 following the collapse of the Ronan Point flats in East London and the line closed completely. Few realised at the time that the Wroxham/Aylsham stretch would later become the trackbed for a narrow-gauge railway (chapter 5).

5
Preserved Lines In Norfolk

Wells & Walsingham Light Railway
North Norfolk Railway
Mid-Norfolk Railway
Bure Valley Railway

Lt Cmdr Roy Francis sits at the controls of his unique 2-6-0 + 0-6-2 Garratt steam locomotive 'Norfolk Hero' prior to a regular passenger run along the longest 10¼ inch gauge railway in the world. (Author)

Wells & Walsingham Light Railway

When the narrow-gauge railway from Wells to Walsingham opened in 1982 it was an immediate success. Preliminary work to re-open the line had started in 1979, including the obtaining of the necessary Light Railway Order from the Department of Transport.

The promoters of the Wells & Walsingham Light Railway (W&WLR) had a lot of hard work to do. Four miles of 10¼ inch narrow-gauge track needed to be laid, fences and bridges repaired and years of neglect put right. Near Walsingham, a cutting had been filled in with rubbish and had to be dug out again! Even so, services began on schedule on 6th April 1982, the day after the Light Railway Order was granted, making it the longest 10¼ inch narrow-gauge railway in the world.

Initially, trains comprised an articulated set of four open carriages hauled by an 0-6-0 side tank locomotive named *Pilgrim*, built specially for the line by David King Engineering of North Walsham. *Pilgrim* had two 6 inch by 4 inch cylinders and a working steam pressure of 125 lbs per square inch. For its size it coped well with its four well-filled coaches over the four miles to Walsingham, which included a climb of 1 in 29.

The line proved to be a strong tourist attraction and it was soon realised that further motive power was needed. In July 1985 an 0-6-0 petrol-driven locomotive to be named *Weasel* was purchased from Alan Keef Limited and this provided a short-term solution. At the same time, bearing in mind that many people prefer steam, thought was given as to how to provide a steam locomotive adequate for the job. Problems with *Pilgrim* had shown that a conventional steam locomotive was not adequate and a totally different approach was needed.

The solution came following consultations with Neil Simkins, a consulting engineer from Ashby-de-la-Zouch, with the result that an unusual and unique design was considered. The idea was to build a Garratt type of locomotive which had twice the power of *Pilgrim*, to be achieved by providing two engine units which would be articulated and have a cradle slung between them carrying the boiler, firebox and cab. The design was agreed and, following a successful share flotation plus a grant from the English Tourist Board, construction began in the autumn of 1985. It was a very proud day for Lt Cmdr Roy Francis, who had pioneered the W&WLR, and the many friends of the railway when, on 18th October 1986, the Viscountess Coke of Holkham named the new locomotive *Norfolk Hero*.

Recent developments at the W&WLR include conversion of the petrol-driven locomotive *Weasel* to diesel hydraulic with a redesigned bodywork, and the building of a new engine shed on the Walsingham side of the signal box at Wells. Also two smart covered coaches with padded seats have been added to the rolling stock. In addition, plans are in hand to reduce the 1 in 29 gradient on part of the journey. The W&WLR is open seven days a week and journeys may be commenced at either end.

The North Norfolk Railway

When the railway between Sheringham and Melton Constable closed at the end of 1964, numerous ambitious schemes were put forward by the M&GN Preservation Society to save certain of the old lines. The initial ideas proved impractical but the society was eventually able to raise enough money to save the three-mile section from Weybourne to the station boundary at

Weybourne station around the time of closure by British Rail in 1964. Despite the endeavours of the M&GN Preservation Society, BR removed all the track and sidings at Weybourne before the Society could raise sufficient capital. (Lens of Sutton)

An exhibit worth seeing at Sheringham is Gresley buffet car no 51769 originally built by the LNER at York. The car is in first class condition with restoration having been masterminded by volunteer Steve Allen. (Author)

Sheringham. Unfortunately, the paperwork took time and by completion, demolition contractors had already removed all the track and sidings at Weybourne and had worked some way towards Sheringham.

In 1967, British Rail abandoned the original Sheringham station in favour of a halt on the other side of the main road. The society immediately took a lease on the building and transferred its activities there. The prospect of operating a preserved railway had now become more practical and to this end a private company, Central Norfolk Enterprises Limited, was formed. Two years later in 1969 it became the North Norfolk Railway Company (NNR) and went public, initially raising £14,000.

During this time volunteers had been relaying the track and sidings ready for the locomotives and rolling stock already purchased. These included two steam locomotives, two Diesel Railbuses and a set of 1924 ex-King's Cross Suburban Quad-art

The W. H. Smith bookstall at Sheringham is on long-term loan from the National Railway Museum, having stood for many years on the concourse of London's Waterloo station. (Author)

coaches. In 1976 the NNR was granted a Light Railway Order by the Department of the Environment and a regular passenger service between Sheringham and Weybourne was soon to follow.

Thanks to the hard work of many volunteers, and in addition to help given through the Manpower Services Commission schemes, further track was laid from Weybourne to Kelling Camp Halt (reached in 1983) and Holt. The original 1887 Holt station disappeared with the building of a town bypass many years ago, so the NNR built its own station just off the A148 Cromer-Fakenham road. Holt station is today the southern terminus of the NNR and it has also become the home of a Midland Railway signal box. This came from Upper Portland on the Nottingham-Worksop line following a period in store at the Midland Railway Centre.

Further work carried out has included the restoration of locomotives – including the popular 0-6-0 ex-GER J15 no 7564 originally built in 1912. Passenger coaches too form an

Holt station, southern terminus of the North Norfolk Railway, on a wet day. The original 1887 Holt station disappeared many years ago when the town's bypass was built. (Author)

important part of the railway and these include two 'Brighton Belle' cars which have been converted to become locomotive-hauled, one of which has been adapted for use by disabled travellers. Another is Gresley buffet car no 51769 originally built by the LNER at York in 1937. This car is in superb condition and a fine example of restoration work masterminded by volunteer Steve Allen. On platform 2 at Sheringham can be seen a W.H.Smith bookstall which once stood on the concourse of London's Waterloo station.

The past is certainly not forgotten. The Midland & Great Northern Joint Railway Society was founded when the M&GN closed in 1959 so that part of that railway might be preserved for the 'pleasure, enjoyment and education of future generations'. One of the society's main roles is to preserve and restore to active use the locomotives and coaches which it owns, an aspect in which many members play an active part. The M&GN Society meets twice yearly and produces a quarterly journal called *Joint Line*.

The Mid-Norfolk Railway

Over the past few years there have been numerous plans to restore the line from Wymondham northwards towards Fakenham where track remains in situ from Wymondham to North Elmham. Between 1989 and 1995 trains ran over a one and a half mile relaid stretch of track at County School station, with the intention that it should ultimately link with North Elmham. This did not materialise but, in 1998, the Mid-Norfolk Railway (MNR) had an offer accepted by the BR Property Board for the five and a half mile stretch from North Elmham to Dereham. The Preservation Trust was also able to reverse the neglect at County School station since its earlier 1990 restoration by re-opening it as a museum and tea-room.

When the MNR acquire the link between Dereham and Elmham, track will be relaid on to County School which will eventually become the interim MNR terminus from

Dereham station, today the headquarters of the Mid-Norfolk Railway Preservation Trust, photographed in October 1998. The MNR plans to run trains between Dereham and Wymondham. (Author)

59

Yaxham station between Wymondham and Dereham remains in a well preserved state. The line closed to regular passenger services in October 1969 although a single line terminating at North Elmham survived for freight purposes. (Author)

Wymondham. The proposal has the blessing of Norfolk County Council which hopes that eventually trains can reach Fakenham.

The whole Dereham/Wymondham line was passed for freight in July 1998 and the Mid-Norfolk Railway's first success came when a trial run of army vehicles used the track. A 350-ton train from Eastleigh comprising special Warfleet and Warwell wagons, an EW&S observation coach and stores wagon, was hauled from Wymondham by MNR class 20 diesel no 20069 and tailed by Railfreight's class 47 no 47241 *Halewood Silver Jubilee*. At Dereham the train was loaded with five armoured vehicles by members of the 9th/12th Royal Lancers (Prince of Wales's) from nearby barracks. The success of that train paved the way to run regular army freight services. Already further military trains have used the line, one carrying 800 tons of stores unloaded in Dereham yard.

A reminder of earlier times found on the platform at Yaxham with tempting offers of rail travel including trips to east coast resorts. (Author)

County School station, October 1998. The Mid-Norfolk Railway Preservation Trust plan that this station will become their northern terminus at a future date. (Author)

Also in 1998 the MNR purchased the line from Dereham to Wymondham. Passenger services had already commenced between Dereham and Yaxham in 1996. During the author's visit to Dereham in October 1998, a class 122 diesel 'bubble-car' no 55006 was providing regular passenger services and there were occasional demonstration freight trains. Passenger trains will reach Wymondham from Yaxham when the remaining section of this line has been upgraded to passenger standards. At Wymondham a temporary station has been built in anticipation, to be called Wymondham Abbey, and a 150 yard footpath is planned to link the MNR and Railtrack stations. When completed, this will surely boost the MNR's current successes.

The Bure Valley Railway

Work on the Bure Valley Railway (BVR) began in 1989 with the task of constructing a nine mile 15 inch-gauge track between

The Bure Valley Railway's 2-6-2 'Blickling Hall' hauls seven passenger coaches out of Aylsham on the nine mile 15 inch gauge track towards Wroxham. (Author)

Work at the Bure Valley Railway during October 1998 included the laying of new three-way track with assistance from 'Little Titan', a Cheeseman steam crane. (Picture courtesy Paul Conibeare, Bure Valley Railway).

Aylsham and Wroxham. The project was part funded by the English Tourist Board and the Department of the Environment. The railway opened the following year on 10th July 1990. The route includes 17 bridges and a 105 foot girder bridge over the river Bure at Buxton. Construction of the BVR required a tunnel under the Aylsham bypass.

The headquarters of the BVR is at Aylsham where the station has four platforms. There is covered accommodation for passengers as well as the rolling stock. Travelling from Aylsham, the first intermediate station is Brampton with the village to the left. The station at Buxton was built on the site of the former GER Buxton Lamas station which closed to passengers in September 1952. The last intermediate station is at Coltishall, another former GER station site and home during the Second World War to 292 Squadron RAF commanded by Squadron Leader Douglas Bader. It remains an RAF base currently equipped with Jaguar fighters.

The BVR today boasts five steam engines, one diesel hydraulic engine, one diesel mechanical shunting engine and a steam crane named *Little Titan*. It has 20 fully enclosed bogie saloon cars, two specially built cars for use by wheelchairs and two four-wheel passenger brake vans. During 2002 the BVR invested heavily in four more new wheelchair accessible coaches. This allows the railway to have coaches with wheelchair access on every train. A long-term project is the construction of a new steam loco, the scale Great Central 2-8-0. This will see a lot of use around the Aylsham station site during the *Day out with Thomas* events, which are held each year at the end of May and September.

The Bure Valley Railway's success is undoubted. During 2002 it carried approximately 127,500 passengers, an increase of around 10% over two years. The route is paralleled throughout its length by the Bure Valley Walk and cycleway, which gives enthusiasts plenty of photographic opportunities.

6
Norfolk/Suffolk Borders And A Steam Museum

Tivetshall to Beccles
Swaffham to Thetford
Thetford to Bury St Edmunds
Bressingham Live Steam Museum

Tivetshall station, on the main Ipswich to Norwich line, when it was a junction for the Waveney Valley Railway (Tivetshall to Beccles) which closed to passengers in 1953. (Lens of Sutton)

Tivetshall to Beccles

Many relics of the The Waveney Valley Railway (WVR) remain to be found. Tivetshall station buildings have gone – 'flattened almost overnight', bemoaned a local enthusiast – but Pulham Market station is certainly still there. The owner, proud of his

Pulham Market station building which has been converted to a private residence. The signal came from Tivetshall station. (Author)

possession, has renovated the building much to its former standard. At the end of the platform stands the signal that in days gone by controlled the branch out of Tivetshall. Only the arm was missing but this has been replaced by another from nearby Mellis.

There were further discoveries along the route. Pulham St Mary station building was demolished in the 1970s yet not far away, along Doctor's Lane, stands Crossing Cottage where level-crossing gates from Tivetshall span the former track. Starston (which closed in 1866!) has survived as a private dwelling known as 'Crossing Gates'. Much of the original woodwork has survived. The building at Harleston, owned by a builder, stands in the town but without its canopy. Geldeston station building and platform are in industrial use.

Beccles was once an important junction with numerous sidings, sheds, four facing platforms and (in 1902) a staff of 55. Today there is only one single line and the station is unstaffed. Where Waveney Valley trains once called, weeds and rubble have replaced the track. Early ideas for a line along the Waveney

Not far from Pulham St Mary this level-crossing gate from Tivetshall has been preserved at a former crossing cottage. (Author)

Valley came in 1846, proposing a route from Diss to serve Lowestoft and Yarmouth via Bungay and Beccles, giving the coastal towns a better service from London than was then possible via Norwich. This did not materialise and local folk, concerned that they might not get a railway, planned a line from Tivetshall Junction, to the north of Diss, direct to Harleston. Initial approval was only from Tivetshall to Bungay, a prosperous river navigation terminal and market town. Trains eventually reached Beccles on 2nd March 1863, on the same day the WVR was formally absorbed into the Great Eastern Railway (GER).

Throughout the line's life there were four to seven trains daily each way. Yet the number of intermediate stations was not justified with Starston and Redenhall closing as early as 1866 and Wortwell in 1878. During the First World War, a long siding was built at Pulham Market to serve an airship base, an area which was used again in the Second World War by the RAF. The latter period proved the line's busiest time, with Earsham alone handling some 200,000 tons of military stores to supply the numerous air bases in the area.

Starston station on the Waveney Valley line lasted only six years closing in 1866! The building became a crossing cottage until closure of the line. It has today been tastefully converted to a private residence. (Author)

After the Second World War, traffic declined to such an extent that passenger services were withdrawn on 5th January 1953, with freight following in stages to finally close on 19th April 1965.

Swaffham to Thetford

Despite financial difficulties, the first section of a line from Swaffham to Thetford to open was between Thetford (Roudham Junction) and Watton. Goods traffic began on 28th January 1869 with passenger traffic following on 18th October. The Thetford & Watton Railway (T&W) Bill had been approved by Parliament on 16th July 1866 with authority to raise £45,000 to construct the nine miles of track which would link Watton with the main line from Ely to Norwich.

Wretham & Hockham station building, now a private residence, on the former line from Swaffham to Thetford which closed in 1964. (Author)

The remaining link to be constructed by the Watton and Swaffham Railway was approved in 1869, the year trains reached Watton, with an authorised capital of £62,000. Nine and a half miles of track were needed to link with the GER line from King's Lynn to Dereham. With finance still in short supply, it was not until 20th September 1875 that the line opened for goods traffic, with passenger trains following on 15th November. In 1898 both companies became part of the GER.

Prior to the First World War the area, known as the Breckland, was used for extensive military training with the transport of horses and large quantities of weapons and supplies by rail. By 1921, Roudham Junction, because of its isolated position, had lost its importance and main-line trains were no longer stopping there. The station closed officially on 1st May 1932. However, other stations were less neglected. In the years before the Second World War, Wretham & Hockham regularly won prizes for the upkeep of its station. When the war came, a RAF base was built alongside the track at Watton and a cement centre was

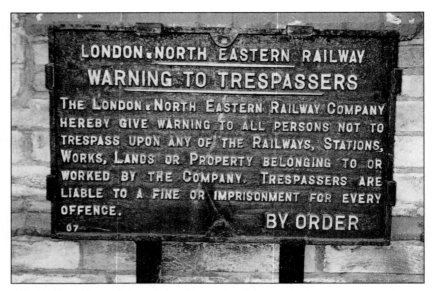

A reminder of the London & North Eastern Railway found on the former Wretham & Hockham station platform. (Author)

established near Roudham for airfield construction.

After 1945 the line returned to a quiet role but, despite the use of diesel multiple-units, the Beeching Report brought services to an end. Passenger services ceased on 15th June 1964 although freight continued between Swaffham and Watton for almost another year, with Home Hale providing useful sugar-beet traffic. Perhaps the best recollection of the line for many was of the station name together with an outline of a locomotive cut into the hedge by staff at Watton.

Swaffham station lives on today as a community centre known as the Merle Boddy Centre. It was opened by Gillian Shepherd MP on 16th May 1988 and named after Merle Boddy, a Mayoress four times, who died in 1987. The listed building has been restored with the help of Manpower Services, which at times had to have bricks hand made to match the existing ones from the 19th century.

Thetford to Bury St Edmunds

The Bury St Edmunds & Thetford Railway Company began services along its 13 mile route on 1st March 1876, working with a speed limit of 30 mph and a weight limit of 40 tons on locomotives. Officially, trains terminated at Thetford Bridge to the south of the town although a spur to the north existed linking via GER tracks to the Roudham Junction/Swaffham line.

The company suffered financial problems and it was no surprise when the GER took over the line. Two World Wars brought about an increase of traffic with Barnham seeing much of the activity. During the First World War a large military camp was opened in the area and for the Second World War special sidings were built for an ICI factory, with further sidings catering for one of the country's largest bomb dumps. The latter gave the line much traffic with wagons handling some 720,000 tons during the war years, with many 'secret trains' leaving during the night.

The GER Thetford Bridge station, probably during the First World War as troops board a train. The line opened in 1876. (Lens of Sutton)

71

Thetford Bridge after closure in 1960 when the Thetford to Bury St Edmunds line came to an end. For a time the building became a youth hostel but this closed in 1971. (Lens of Sutton)

After the war, traffic reduced dramatically and on 8th June 1953 passenger services came to an end. At Bury St Edmunds there were 'celebrations' to mark the end with a funeral (with coffin), a procession of 'weeping mourners' attired in Victorian dress, an old steam engine and a manual fire pump manned by 19th century firemen. Detonators were fired on the track, streamers were thrown and wreaths decorated the engine as the *Thetford Flyer* made its last passenger journey.

The closure of freight services in June 1960 finally brought the line to an end. When on 27th June 1960, BR J17 locomotive no 65578 moved slowly out of Bury St Edmunds station for the last time, pulling two wagons and a brake van, there was no big send-off. The *Bury Free Press* of 1st July 1960 reported:

'Few people in Bury seemed to know about the goods train. There were no other passengers except railway enthusiast,

The derelict remains of Thetford Bridge station, October 1998, which could be found in a council yard just below a roundabout where part of the trackbed was used to build a section of bypass. Plans were in hand to demolish the building. (Author)

W. F. White, the Borough Treasurer, who was just going along for the ride – plus a reporter. At Thetford not a soul was in sight except 14-year old Patrick Spruce, a loco spotter, who had come to take pictures of the train he would see no more'.

Bressingham Live Steam Museum

Bressingham Live Steam Museum is a haven for locomotive enthusiasts, yet it is known not only for its steam museum but also its enchanting gardens. This was an interest started by owner Alan Bloom with his young family in 1946 when he purchased Bressingham Hall Farm to run a nursery business. At first not all went well but slowly their efforts won through.

The first interest in steam came in 1961 when Alan Bloom, already interested in restoring an old 1912 Burrell traction

BR Standard Class 7 Pacific locomotive no 70013, 'Oliver Cromwell',
admired by onlookers outside Norwich station, August 1968, during a break
in its journey from Carlisle to Bressingham. (Photographed by
G. R. Mortimer – picture courtesy Bressingham Steam Museum)

engine, purchased another Burrell which he named *Bertha*. This
was soon put to steam and it was immediately noticeable that
visitors to the nursery were taking more than a passing interest.
By the end of the year eight engines stood in the yard, most of
them derelict and awaiting restoration.

By 1965 the enthusiasm spread to railway locomotives when a
750 yard 9½ inch narrow-gauge track became operational,
carrying passengers alongside the garden. Half a mile of 2 foot
gauge track followed, the rolling stock purchased from a slate
quarry in North Wales where steam had given way to diesel
lorries. The trains, hauled initially by a little 0-4-0 Hunslet
named *George Sholto*, were so well patronised that track
extensions were soon necessary.

The idea of a steam museum to house standard-gauge
locomotives came in 1967, soon after the Beeching cuts had

The 4-6-0 Royal Scot locomotive no 6100 was built privately in 1927. It was exhibited in the USA at the 1933 Chicago Exposition Fair. It later covered over 11,000 miles fitted with a warning bell and electric headlamp to meet USA regulations. (Picture courtesy Bressingham Steam Museum)

taken full effect. At first, locomotives offered were out of reach financially but when British Rail later suggested that engines could be sent out on permanent loan to private organisations or museums, then Alan Bloom acted. During the winter of 1967/8 a shed covering 12,500 square feet was erected and when completed was passed as suitable. The first locomotive to arrive was *William Francis*, the last remaining 0-4-0 + 0-4-0T Beyer-Peacock Garratt in Britain, a unique articulated engine, similar in design to that used on the narrow-gauge Wells & Walsingham Railway. Another destined for Bressingham was *Thundersley*, a 4-4-2 tank built in 1909 for the London, Tilbury & Southend Railway, which was housed at Attleborough for several weeks whilst being restored by members of the Norfolk Railway Society.

When the BR Standard Class 7 Pacific locomotive, no 70013, *Oliver Cromwell*, arrived in August 1968 there was great excitement. This engine had been selected to head the last steam-hauled train by British Rail and the trip had been made from Liverpool to Carlisle. From Carlisle it steamed through the night across country to Norwich from where it later travelled to Diss station to be loaded for road transport. At Bressingham no time was lost and *Oliver Cromwell* was in steam and motion along a short stretch of track within only five weeks.

Oliver Cromwell has since taken its turn in giving demonstration footplate rides. Today there are a total of 14 standard-gauge locomotives and in addition there are several narrow-gauge locomotives hauling coaches on three separate routes totalling in all some five miles. On the 50 open days each summer, around 80,000 people of all ages take rides around the nursery by the lake or the woods. The 120,000 annual visitors can also see a collection of steam engines – some in motion – as well as a large museum housing two Royal Coaches together with many items of railway interest. What began as Alan Bloom's hobby in 1961 has truly become the most comprehensive live steam museum in Europe.

7
Suffolk/Essex Borders

Closure of the line from Marks Tey to Sudbury has been planned by BR on more than one occasion but, thanks to efforts on behalf of commuters, the line has remained open. A diesel railbus waits at the station in earlier BR days. (Lens of Sutton)

A line from Marks Tey to Sudbury opened on 2nd July 1849. When the first train left Marks Tey, the locomotive dislodged the triumphal arch, with the result that it carried the laurels and other decorations round its chimney and dome throughout the journey to Sudbury!

In order that the branch could cross the narrow valley of the river Colne before climbing steeply towards the Mount Bures summit, a viaduct some 70 feet high had to be built. It was originally intended that the Chappel Viaduct should be of

Sudbury station in October 1998, considerably diminished from its earlier state. The station's footbridge is currently in use at the East Anglian Railway Museum at Chappel & Wakes Colne. (Author)

timber construction, probably on brick piers, but plans were changed when it was discovered that bricks could be made locally and cheaply at Bures.

The laying of a foundation stone for the viaduct proved quite an occasion. On the day, 14th September 1847, a bottle containing coins of the time was placed under the stone but, within hours, the stone had been removed and the coins stolen. Were it not for the keen eyes of a barmaid at the nearby Rose and Crown who spotted a new coin, the culprit, a Norwich bricklayer, might have got away with it.

The Colne Valley & Halstead Railway was incorporated by an Act of 30th June 1856 and given permission to build from Chappel to Halstead. After difficult negotiations with the Eastern Counties Railway (ECR), owners of the Marks Tey to Sudbury branch, it was agreed that a junction could be built at Chappel for a payment of £1,500. In 1859 a further Act authorised the Colne Valley company to extend from Halstead

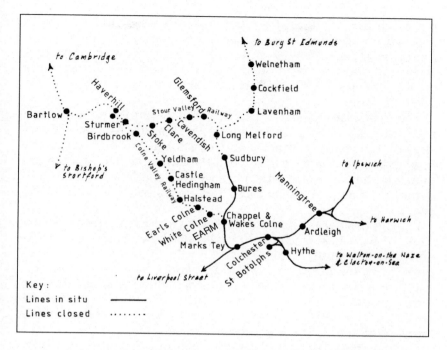

to Haverhill. The section from Chappel to Halstead opened on 16th April 1860 and the remainder of the line to Haverhill opened on 10th May 1863.

Yet another company now emerged, the Sudbury & Clare Railway, empowered to build via Long Melford. But as soon as powers were obtained, the ECR took over and immediately sought extended powers to build from Sudbury to Shelford on the London-Cambridge main line, plus a branch from Long Melford to Bury St Edmunds. At the same time, the Colne Valley company, anxious to be independent from the ECR, sought approval for a line to Cambridge and, in the other direction, a line to Colchester.

A bitter struggle between the two powers ensued but the Colne Valley Bill was rejected and, on 6th August 1861, the ECR received approval to go ahead. Further changes were imminent, for in August 1862 an amalgamation of companies including the ECR came about and the GER came into being. The Act also renewed the authorisation for the proposed ECR lines to proceed, in addition to a connecting line at Haverhill between the original Stour Valley and Colne Valley railways. The first section to open between Shelford and Haverhill began services on 1st June 1865 with three trains each way on weekdays and one on Sundays.

The remaining lines from Haverhill to Sudbury and from Melford to Bury St Edmunds followed on 9th August 1865. A new two-platform station was necessary at Sudbury since the line had to be diverted in a westerly direction. The old single-platform terminus became part of the goods yard and was demolished as recently as 1985/6 when a store was built on the site.

During the period prior to the First World War, the lines saw some of their best traffic with seven weekday passenger trains daily on the stretch from Marks Tey to Sudbury. There were through trains between Cambridge and Clacton via Sudbury and through carriages between Liverpool Street and Sudbury on four trains daily. The war brought little reduction in traffic and on 1st October 1914, Chappel was given the name better known today, 'Chappel & Wakes Colne'.

During the 1920s rail traffic continued quite healthily although economies became necessary. These included the removal of various signal boxes, to be replaced in some instances by ground frames. Many excursion trains remained in existence but the through carriages from Liverpool Street to Sudbury gave way to a single slip carriage removed daily at Marks Tey.

When the Second World War came, the situation changed dramatically. Passenger services were reduced although freight services remained active. When the Allied bomber offensive began, with airfields being established throughout the area, the lines assumed new importance. The line from Cambridge to Chappel & Wakes Colne took on extra traffic as rubble was carried for the construction of a new airfield at Wormingford. When completed, a petrol depot was built at Chappel & Wakes Colne and trains were bringing high-octane petrol for the aircraft twice daily. Troop movements also figured largely in the line's traffic and it was not long before 2-8-0 'Austerity'

Glemsford on the Stour Valley line which closed to passengers in March 1967. Many station buildings along this attractive route have today been converted to private properties. (Lens of Sutton)

locomotives were seen in use. There were frequent delays because of air raids or flying bombs but no actual damage was recorded.

Changes came in 1959 when British Rail announced a modernisation programme. Steam was scrapped to be replaced by Diesel Railbuses and Multiple Units. Although passenger traffic showed some improvement, it was not enough to overcome the increasing losses being incurred on these rural lines. Nobody was really surprised when closure came on 10th April 1961 to the passenger service between Long Melford and Bury St Edmunds, where traffic had become very light.

The passenger service on the Colne Valley line was soon to follow but not before sharp reactions were expressed. Haverhill Urban District Council sent a telegram to Dr Beeching protesting most strongly at the proposal 'to sever the town's rail link with London at a time when the town was planning to expand'. Despite such efforts, the last passenger train ran from

Clare station before closure in 1967. The station building and platforms have been incorporated within a country park centre surrounded by lawns. (Lens of Sutton)

Chappel & Wakes Colne to Haverhill on 31st December 1961. When in April 1965 the British Railways Board gave notice of their intention to close the remaining line from Marks Tey to Cambridge, there was again a vigorous reaction.

Total closure was planned for 31st December 1966 but, bearing in mind the views of the East Anglian Transport Users' Consultative Committee, the Minister of Transport refused permission for the Sudbury to Marks Tey section to be closed because of commuter needs and also development of the town at Sudbury. With regard to the Sudbury to Cambridge passenger service, matters were further delayed while local councils considered the possibility of providing annual subsidy guarantees. These were sought by the railway authorities

Chappel & Wakes Colne station on the branch between Marks Tey and Sudbury. The buildings are a good example of Victorian architecture and the station is today the centre for the East Anglian Railway Museum. (Lens of Sutton)

following examination of the track which was found to be in a poor condition. The councils were concerned at the high costs involved and, not unexpectedly, withdrew support. The line from Sudbury to Shelford closed entirely on 6th March 1967.

In 1968 BR again published proposals for the closure of the Marks Tey to Sudbury line following a decision from the Minister of Transport to discontinue its subsidy. There was once more a considerable outcry from the public and for some years no decision was taken. In June 1972 the Minister for the Environment announced the line would close in July 1974 if the local councils would not support continuation. In 1974 there was an energy crisis with the possibility of petrol rationing, with the result that, in the interests of the local community, the line remained open.

Sudbury has become a single-platform 'bus stop type' station. There has been talk in the past about the possibility of electrification but this seems as far away as ever. At least during

Chappel & Wakes Colne station in GER days. Before the Beeching cuts it was possible to catch a train from Chappel to Haverhill along the Colne Valley. (Lens of Sutton)

1998 the 38-year old veteran 'Bubble Cars' used on the branch were replaced by a Class 153 single car hired from Anglia Railways.

Many traces of the closed lines can be found today. When visited several years ago, Welnetham station building, now privately owned, had a short awning and the station wall was still in situ. The owner remarked on the splendid soil found in his garden. The station-master in his time had tired of the local clay and had arranged for quantities of fine Fen soil to be railed in by truck to take its place. One of the perks of the job, he obviously considered.

The ornate cast-iron toilet that once adorned the platform at Cockfield station now stands proudly (as an exhibit only!) at the East Anglian Railway Museum at Chappel & Wakes Colne. Similarly, Lavenham station building and a nearby overbridge have survived with the area now used industrially.

On the Stour Valley line, the station buildings and platforms

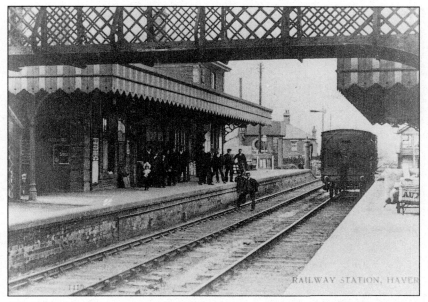

Haverhill, seen here c1910 with its complement of staff, was at one time where the rival Stour Valley and Colne Valley routes met. In 1862, when the GER came into being, a connecting line at Haverhill was built joining the two railways. (Lens of Sutton)

at Clare stand virtually complete, incorporated within a country park centre. Nearby is a goods shed and a short section of track and inside can be found a former British Rail box van. The shed is today a museum where many old local railway photographs can be seen.

The closed Colne Valley line from Chappel & Wakes Colne to Haverhill has similarly left reminders. Earls Colne station buildings have survived and are used today by a local firm. Sible & Castle Hedingham station was purchased on closure by a local woodworking company and in the early 1970s the buildings were due to be demolished by a bulldozer to make way for a new warehouse – but this never happened.

Also in the early 1970s, another group of dedicated enthusiasts obtained a lease on the vacant goods yard, goods

A photographic view through the supporting arches of the 1,066 foot Chappel Viaduct which required approximately 7,000,000 bricks for its construction in the 1840s. (Author)

shed, signal box and station buildings at an intermediate station on the surviving Marks Tey to Sudbury branch.

Both these events were to have far-reaching effects in the two separate areas in the years to come. No doubt in the past many thought that steam had gone for good at Chappel & Wakes Colne or in the Colne Valley, but they were to be proved very wrong.

8
A Railway Museum And A Line Preserved

The East Anglian Railway Museum
The Colne Valley Railway

The East Anglian Railway Museum

The Stour Valley Preservation Society was formed on 24th September 1968. Its intention was to preserve all or part of the line from Sudbury to Shelford which had closed the previous year. This was an ambitious project and, with funds in short supply, it resulted in failure and the line was lost. In 1970, with the remaining stretch from Sudbury to Marks Tey still under threat of closure, the society found it necessary to form an associated company in order to negotiate with British Rail for take-over of the branch and the Branch Line Preservation Society Company Ltd was formed. The primary objective was to safeguard the Marks Tey-Sudbury branch although events were to prove that the line remained open. In December 1970 the society formed its headquarters at Chappel & Wakes Colne station where a lease was negotiated on the redundant goods yard, goods shed, signal box and station buildings.

After some three months of very hard work, track and pointwork over a third of a mile had been relaid and a locomotive, 0-6-0ST Gunby, was hauling a GER contractor's van loaded with passengers! Further rolling stock and locomotives arrived, the main attraction proving to be the Southern Railway class S.15 locomotive, no 30841. Financial assistance to restore this fine engine came from a well known Suffolk brewing company and it was fitting the locomotive should be named *Greene King*.

Progress continued with buildings restored and part of the station building became a bookshop – proving a major source of

The ornate cast-iron toilet to be found by the museum's restoration shed and workshop (as an exhibit only!) came from Cockfield station on the line from Long Melford to Bury St Edmunds. (Author)

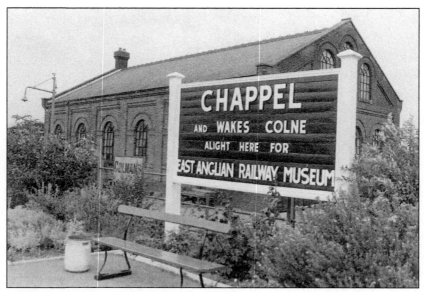

Chappel & Wakes Colne station is not only an intermediate station between Marks Tey and Sudbury, it is also a registered museum as well as an active repair and restoration depot. (Author)

income. The GER-designed class N7 arrived for a complete rebuild. The N7, built in 1924, was the last ever locomotive to be built at the GER's Stratford Works. The GER had been absorbed into the LNER and Stratford subsequently became a maintenance depot. The N7 spent much of its life in the Liverpool Street suburban area but in 1962 it was withdrawn and stored for ten years before being towed to Chappel where it was completely stripped down and rebuilt to BR main line standards.

The late 1970s proved a difficult time for the society. A number of the locomotives, notably *Greene King*, went to other locations. Attendances at the station site dwindled and membership participation lessened. However, the acquisition of a footbridge from Sudbury station in the early 1980s was a boost to morale since visitors could now cross the BR line independently and the expense of a BR crossing keeper was no longer necessary.

The East Anglian Railway Museum. To the far left is the platform for Great Eastern Railway services. To the right beyond the former down platform, special steam days at the museum prove very popular. (Author)

Interest was further revived when the society attempted to run steam regularly on the branch on Sundays. Plans to steam between Chappel & Wakes Colne and Marks Tey were declined by BR for various reasons, so interest turned elsewhere on the site. Track was relaid along platform 2 to allow steam running and, following the purchase of an adjacent plot of land, an engine restoration shed and workshop were built. The site acquired its present-day name of The East Anglian Railway Museum (EARM) in late 1985. It obtained charitable status in 1991.

A signal box, a Grade I listed building, was rescued from Mistley station (on the line to Harwich) for the sum of £5! The box was fully restored to eventually control most of the signalling and the points at the northern end of the site. In 1987 British Rail agreed to sell the station site despite the fact that a pay train service still operated from Colchester to Sudbury.

Today, Chappel & Wakes Colne is not merely a station and a

The 'Chappel North' signal box at the East Anglian Railway Museum came from Mistley at a price of £5! The lamps on the platform are reproductions of the original. (Author)

registered museum but also an active repair and restoration depot. Visitors can find not only restored engines and numerous vintage coaches, but can also see every aspect of repair work, manned largely by volunteers. The popular GER 0-6-2T N7 locomotive is well known in railway circles. After its successful rebuild in 1989 it appeared at a 150 year celebration at Southend hauling a shuttle train. For its high standard of restoration it was awarded the British Coal Steam Heritage Award, an accolade indeed for the museum volunteers at Chappel. The locomotive is currently on long term loan at the North Norfolk Railway and is undergoing a major overhaul. It is hoped that it will re-enter service in spring 2004.

The Sudbury Branch celebrated 150 years in July 1999 with a special vintage train and passengers in Victorian dress. This coincided with the renaming of the branch by its operators, First Great Eastern, as the 'Gainsborough Line' after the artist of that name who lived and worked in Sudbury.

Regrettably, hopes of the Museum lines crossing Chappel viaduct have been dashed due to the vast logistical and operational problems of restricted clearances on the viaduct, and deterioration of the trackbed at the south end which will now only permit the operation of one line of track. The viaduct was crossed, however, by a steam locomotive and train in 2002 when, to the excitement of all, an excursion hauled by Merchant Navy Class locomotive *Canadian Pacific*, called at Chappel & Wakes Colne station for servicing at the Museum.

The Colne Valley Railway

Were it not for the quick thinking of members of the Colne Valley Railway Preservation Society (CVRPS), then Sible & Castle Hedingham station building might have been lost for ever. When the Colne Valley line finally closed to goods traffic in

Hedingham signal box at the Colne Valley Railway, originally built by the GER, was formerly located at Cressing on the Braintree branch. Made redundant by BR in 1977, the box was moved to the CVR in June of that year. (Author)

Pullman cars at the Colne Valley Railway include 'Aquila', once allocated to the Bournemouth Belle service and later sold to the Venice-Simplon Orient Express. Another Pullman is 'Hermione', once part of the Devon Belle Service. (Author)

December 1964, the whole station and goods yard area at Sible & Castle Hedingham was purchased by a local woodworking firm. In the early 1970s the station building, 1861, was due to be demolished since the site was required for a new warehouse.

Such was the good fortune of the CVRPS that when they approached the owner, he agreed to hold back his bulldozer – provided the society could remove the station within six weeks! The target was kept, the building was carefully dismantled – brick by brick.

The project came into existence because of a vision inspired by a walk by two founder members of the society along the overgrown trackbed of the former railway in the summer of 1972. What followed was ten years of relentless hard work by a dedicated group of enthusiasts to recreate what can be seen today.

The first task was to obtain consent for the various planning applications submitted. When agreement was eventually given, work began in earnest in July 1973 to clear the site of almost ten years of overgrown trees and shrubs. The first locomotive arrived in September 1973, an ex-WD 0-6-0 Austerity saddle tank steam locomotive, WD190, built in 1952, causing quite a stir as it wound its way to its new site through the quiet Essex villages in 'full steam' on a massive low loader. The 'driver', the society's Locomotive Superintendent, made sure that the local folk knew it was there by sounding the whistle quite frequently!

The excitement was shortlived for it was to be another two years before a locomotive could be steamed again. Sible & Castle Hedingham station was rebuilt as an exact replica of the past. The work was painstaking but the efforts were justified. The CVRPS consider they are the only private railway to have dismantled, moved and rebuilt a brick station area using voluntary labour only.

During 1974, three more locomotives arrived plus the first items of rolling stock. At the same time, the CVRPS acquired some track which had previously been used at Sudbury station and track laying began. By Easter 1975, about a quarter of a mile had been completed and three points had been laid. There was great excitement when the first 'steam up' was possible, an occasion for which both WD 190 and 0-4-0ST Barrington were brought into service. Footplate rides were given and there were many visitors.

Progress continued with further locomotives and coaches arriving. A building was now required for the second platform plus a signal box. With no suitable authentic building still in existence, the society built its own utilising bricks and materials found from various derelict stations. Any additional bricks necessary were specially made by hand to match the originals. The need for a signal box was solved when one became available at Cressing following electrification of the Braintree to Witham branch. With the platforms completed, the society acquired an ex-GER pattern passenger footbridge from Stowmarket station. It had originated in 1898 and matched its new surroundings splendidly. A final obstacle was overcome when a girder bridge was completed over the river Colne with assistance from the army, the 507 STRE (V) Railway Engineers.

Current rolling stock includes a Pullman car named *Aquila* built in 1951, once allocated to the Bournemouth Belle service and later sold to the Venice-Simplon Orient Express. Another Pullman named *Hermione* was built in 1926, and for a time it was part of the Devon Belle service. Standing on the busy platform and surrounded by so many railway relics of the past, it seems incredible to think that just over 25 years ago, the site was a mere path through the undergrowth.

9
The Mid-Suffolk Light Railway

Haughley to Laxfield
The Mid-Suffolk Light Railway Museum

LNER (ex-GER) 0-6-0 J15 no 65447 leaves Haughley with a mixed passenger/goods set in the early 1950s not long before closure of the Mid-Suffolk Light Railway (MSLR). (Lens of Sutton)

Had the original plans of the independent Mid-Suffolk Light Railway (MSLR) approved in the 1901 Light Railway Order been realised, then a link would have existed between the GER stations of Haughley and Halesworth plus a line between the intermediate stations of Kenton and Westerfield, just north of Ipswich. In addition, the inhabitants of this very rural part of

97

Hudswell-Clarke 0-6-0T locomotive no 2 on the Mid-Suffolk Light Railway approaches Mendlesham bound for Laxfield, probably 1908. The line was originally planned to reach Halesworth on the East Suffolk route but this never materialised. (Lens of Sutton)

Suffolk would have had access to the coast by changing at Halesworth for the Southwold Railway.

Construction of the MSLR began in May 1902 when the Duke of Cambridge cut the first sod at Westerfield at a ceremony which included over 600 guests. Ironically, this section of the line was never to be built. In addition it was soon discovered that marshland on the east-west stretch made it impossible to reach Halesworth from Laxfield. There were also serious financial problems since the project, estimated at £300,000 for the 42 miles of track, ran out of money during the first two years of construction. Hopes still existed to reach Halesworth across the marshland but subsequent deviation routes proved unsuccessful. Similarly, the branch northwards from Westerfield to Kenton failed.

Eventually, on 20th September 1904, a goods service commenced over the 19 miles from Haughley to Laxfield. Small 0-6-0T locomotives had been ordered from Hudswell Clarke of Leeds but when the first was delivered to Haughley, the manufacturers had obviously heard of the line's financial

Aspall station set in open country which never contributed much to passenger traffic. To the left of the picture, Lens of Sutton's bicycle! (Lens of Sutton)

problems. The company kept the engine, named *Haughley*, chained and padlocked to the rails until the first instalment of the purchase price had been received!

Passenger traffic was refused until the line was complete. Progress had been slow with any surpluses needed to meet interest arrears rather than invest in new construction. During 1906 goods trains reached Cratfield towards Halesworth but by May 1907 all work on the line had ceased. The company was declared bankrupt and a receiver was appointed. With the company still anxious to commence passenger services, the board withdrew the earlier stipulation that the line must be completed and agreed services could begin when the track reached a sufficiently high standard.

On 29th September 1908, just over four years after goods services initially commenced, passenger services between Haughley and Laxfield began. Seven old Metropolitan District Railway carriages had been acquired cheaply following electrification of that system. When the first train left Laxfield

Mendlesham station was sited close to the village and became one of the busier stops. During the Second World War the station gained extra traffic from the Mendlesham air base. (Lens of Sutton)

for Haughley soon after 7.35 am on the opening day, there was great excitement from the local people who gathered to cheer the event and enliven the proceedings with exploding detonators. One of the first passengers was Major Daniel, the Receiver. The *East Anglian Daily Times* reported:

> 'a good many tickets were taken, and passengers were eager to enter the train. Only a few minutes behind time the signal was given by the Laxfield station master, and off the train steamed to the accompaniment of hearty cheers from the crowds on the platform, supplemented by the discharging of nearly 30 fog signals.'

There were two or three trains daily and this was to be the

Laxfield station remained the terminus of the MSLR throughout. After closure the station building spent time at Bedfield as a sports pavilion. Today it resides at Mangapps Farm Railway Museum near Burnham-on-Crouch. (Lens of Sutton)

pattern throughout the line's life, with mixed freight and passenger trains becoming a regular sight. Freight remained a useful commodity and included such items as milk churns and boxes of produce which were generally loaded en route. Tuesdays were Ipswich market days and to encourage travel, cheap tickets were available. Loaded cattle trucks became a frequent sight, traffic that had previously travelled by road to the railhead at Framlingham.

During the First World War, there was an incident on the night of 2nd/3rd September 1916, when 13 Zeppelins flew over East Anglia to carry out one of the heaviest raids of the war. Considerable damage was done to GER property especially at Stratford and Liverpool Street, but one bomb scored a direct hit on the MSLR track near Gipping between Haughley and Mendlesham.

The drivers and firemen of the MSLR took great pride in their

A train bound for Haughley arrives at Brockford & Wetheringsett station on the MSLR although the nameboard uses only the name Brockford. (Lens of Sutton)

locomotives which were always highly polished, inside and out. The line continued to give a good service but costs rose and receipts dwindled over the years. When 'grouping' came in 1923 the LNER were at first reluctant to take over the debts of a line that did not pay. After lengthy negotiations, the LNER agreed to meet a proportion of the liabilities and finally on 1st July 1924, the line's independence came to an end.

Whereas changes inevitably took place, the LNER were anxious not to drastically alter the character of this rural railway. One immediate decision was to withdraw the MSLR's locomotives and introduce its own stock. Also, former GER coaches were introduced to replace the MSLR's ex-Midland Railway second-hand stock. A section of worn track was relaid and a number of crossing-keepers were 'retired'. It became the task of the train crew to open and close the gates.

During the 1920s bus competition and private car travel began to erode the line's passenger traffic. The loss was partly

On open land not far from the village of Mendlesham can be found a rather dilapidated old coach, believed to be of GNR origin. During the Second World War it accommodated Italian POWs. (Author)

offset by increasing goods traffic, with sugar beet a reliable source. Commodities brought into the area consisted of coal from the Midlands and mixed freight from Felixstowe and Ipswich docks. Cattle traffic for Ipswich was slowing down and by the late 1930s the special Tuesday trains for market day were abandoned.

In 1933 the LNER seriously contemplated closure of the branch. A proposal to convert the trackbed to a road from Haughley to Laxfield was considered but it was decided that losses would be incurred and the line was saved. In August 1939 there was another attempt to complete the line to Halesworth when the Minister of Transport was approached. The Minister pointed out that powers had expired some 27 years previously and that fresh approval would be needed. When war broke out the following month, the matter was forgotten but the line acquired importance in a different way.

With petrol soon in short supply, passenger traffic grew again although the greatest impact on the line was the eventual basing of American airmen at Mendlesham and Horham airfields. Equipment and ammunition soon became regular freight commodities and to cope with the traffic extra sidings were constructed at Haughley. After the war, passenger traffic increased with schoolchildren making their way to and from Stowmarket Grammar School, with busy loads morning and late afternoon. J15 locomotives stationed at Laxfield became common along the line.

There were few changes when the railways were nationalised in 1948 and the Mid-Suffolk line was to survive another four and a half years as part of BR. During this time the number of passengers dropped and there were times when trains ran empty. Towards the end the line could boast only one season-ticket holder. When closure was listed from 28th July 1952, there was a strong local outcry but the years of near-empty trains had been evidence enough.

The last official train, the 3.55 pm from Haughley, was far from empty. The platforms and temporary refreshment room were packed. Departure was delayed because a connecting train on the main line had broken down and the 3.55 pm, hauled by J15 0-6-0 no 65447, finally left at 4.48 pm. The *Evening Standard* reported that 'villagers from miles around gathered to make the last trip on the last of East Anglia's "puffing-billy" lines, the Mid-Suffolk Railway. Farm workers and railway officials alike sang *Auld Lang Syne* as engine 65447 set out.' It was not quite the end however, for at Laxfield several hundred passengers wanted to return and a final 'unofficial' trip was made.

The Mid-Suffolk Light Railway Museum

In November 1990 a group of enthusiasts met to explore the possibility of creating a railway museum at Wetheringsett, near Stowmarket (just off the A140). Work began in the following year and after long periods of hard work a station building, originally at Mendlesham, was installed on the former Brockford & Wetheringsett cattle-dock platform. In 1994 the Museum won an Ian Allan National Railway Heritage Award.

The former Brockford station is today the site for the Mid-Suffolk Light Railway Museum. The station building came from Mendlesham. (Author)

Further station buildings came from Wilby, Brockford and Haughley. Sections of track were laid and a Hudswell Clarke 0-6-0ST soon stood proudly although much in need of attention. Numerous ex-GER coaches and vans were acquired over the next few years, one of these was four-wheeled coach no 287, built in 1876 and found in a field in 1996 at Acle in Norfolk where it had served as a 'home'. The Mid-Suffolk Light Railway Museum is today a registered charity.

During January 1998 a Ruston & Hornsby 0-4-0 diesel mechanical shunter arrived. Hitherto, shunting had been done by using chains, strops, shackles and a powerful Renault tractor so the 0-4-0's arrival was a welcome relief. When the shunter arrived its condition was filthy. Only with hot water, detergent, hand power and team effort did it reach today's fine standard. After bodywork repairs, it was repainted gloss black.

In July 2002, the MSLR commemorated its 50th year of closure with GER J15 locomotive number 7564, on loan from the North Norfolk Railway, hauling GER coaches.

This four-wheeled coach built in 1876 spent over 80 years as a 'home' at Acle in Norfolk before coming to the Mid-Suffolk Light Railway Museum. (Author)

The three-compartment Smoking Coach no 140 at the Brockford Museum was built by the Great Eastern Railway to an Eastern Counties Railway pattern. (Author)

For the future, plans are in hand to extend the line to about 500 yards and it is hoped to go still further subject to planning permission. Future plans also include extension of facilities and buildings which will free two GER coaches from their duties as shop and refreshment room for restoration, making possible a 'period' train of three of MSLR's own GER coaches. Plans also exist to restore freight wagons to build up a train of four open coal trucks, a GER van, a GER high-sided open and an LNER Toad B. It is hoped in due course to restore the MSLR's Hudswell Clarke 0-6-ST locomotive to good running order.

There is always much to do but, judging by the enthusiasm of its members, the MSLR Company clearly has a future among the region's preserved railways.

10
Branch Lines Of The East Suffolk Railway

Wickham Market to Framlingham
Saxmundham to Aldeburgh

The first trains to run from Yarmouth and Lowestoft to Ipswich were decorated with evergreens. The local press welcomed the service and a report read: 'trains run with great punctuality, and all are loud in their praises of the excellence of the line, and the commodiousness of the new carriages and stations'. There were four trains daily dividing at Beccles linking with the two resorts. With connections available to London, cheap trips to the capital began every Friday. Incorporated into the construction of the

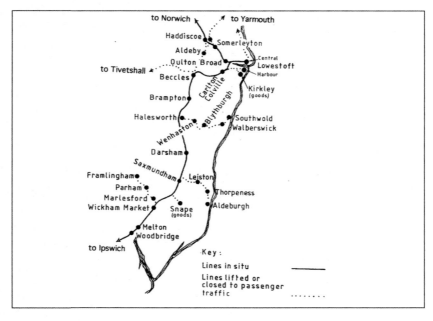

Known locally as 'the bridge that leads nowhere. . .' these remains can be seen from the B1116 just south of Framlingham. The branch finally closed to all traffic in 1965 having succumbed to competition from road traffic. (Author)

East Suffolk Railway were also branch lines to Framlingham, Aldeburgh and Snape. These opened simultaneously with the main line on 1st June 1859. The one and a half mile branch to Snape only ever carried goods. It lasted just over 100 years, closing in March 1960.

Wickham Market to Framlingham

When trains first reached Framlingham from Wickham Market in 1859, church bells were rung throughout the day, a cricket match was played and tea was provided at the Crown Hotel, but there was a problem when a porter fell in front of a train. Luckily the driver was able to stop his engine before any serious injury was done but, since the porter was also the leader of the town band, the concert to celebrate the opening had to be cancelled.

Locomotive no 67230 with brake van and two coaches at Framlingham on 19th July 1952 not long before closure of the line. The station was once a major grain despatch point. (John H. Meredith)

The branch, over five miles in length, was built at an estimated cost of just over £40,000 and initially the weekday service was four trains each way daily and two on Sundays. Passenger traffic was generally poor although when Framlingham College opened in 1864, there were fluctuating increases. Yet Framlingham became an important railhead with the station a major grain despatch point. Also in such times, it was a common sight to see cattle along the road from Laxfield to Framlingham but when the Mid Suffolk Light Railway (MSLR) opened in 1904, this traffic was lost (see chapter 9).

Intermediate stations included Marlesford and Parham. Around the turn of the 20th century a seed mill and corn merchant's depot was established near Marlesford station and subsequently an oil depot was built in the area. Perhaps the station's real claim to fame was when the Duke of Edinburgh's train was housed in the sidings overnight on 2nd May 1956 during his East Anglian tour of that year. There was great excitement locally when a highly-polished B1 4-6-0 locomotive,

Framlingham station building, October 1998. The building has become a Bed Bazaar as well as a showroom for quality British motorcycles where one of the station's original ornamental brackets can still be seen. (Author)

far grander than anything seen for years, hauled the Royal Train along the branch. The only other locomotives of note were usually Claud Hamilton 4-4-0s which were used to haul occasional seaside excursions from Framlingham, with Felixstowe a popular destination.

In the 1920s between Marlesford and Parham, Hacheston Halt appeared, serving little other purpose than to combat growing competition from local buses. Parham, which opened with the line in 1859, achieved importance during the Second World War when petrol and bombs were handled at the station en route to a nearby airfield. Wickham Market station survives although it is more than two miles from the town.

The Framlingham branch line closed to regular passenger traffic on 3rd November 1952. Speed restrictions and a badly-sited terminal station had spelt doom to the branch which eventually succumbed to road competition. Goods services continued for a further twelve and a half years with a daily freight calling at all stations except Parham. The traffic, mainly of grain, coal and beet, survived until 19th April 1965 when the line closed to all traffic.

Wickham Market, on the main East Suffolk line, was reduced to the status of an unstaffed halt on 6th March 1967. The station building on the long down platform is still there. The staggered up platform is no longer used because of line singling and there are traces of bays and also ramps which were used during the Second World War to load tanks into railway wagons. Not far away on the A12, Marlesford station building exists as a private residence.

Framlingham station building survives as a sales outlet for quality British motorcycles. Andy Tiernan, the proprietor, took great pride in showing an old station pillar with its original ornamental brackets still supporting one of the girders from the platform building. Locals recalled that when the engine shed was demolished many years ago, it was hauled down by a locomotive pulling a steel hawser which had been tied around the brickwork!

Saxmundham to Aldeburgh

With a branch already approved from Saxmundham to Leiston, the people of Aldeburgh wanted the line continued to serve their town. The company agreed in principle and a meeting was held in March 1859 to discuss the details. Sir Samuel Peto agreed to bear the cost and said he would lease the line for 21 years. During this time he expected Aldeburgh to expand, thus the line would pay for itself.

The ESR had provided the initial three and a half mile stretch to Leiston at the request of Richard Garrett, an ESR director. Garrett was also owner of Leiston's world-famous engineering works established in 1778, noted for its farm and road transport vehicles. In later years, Richard Garrett Ltd produced locomotive parts for Beyer Peacock locomotives which were used worldwide. With good local employment prospects, Leiston had grown and by 1851 had reached a population of over 1,500 inhabitants. The cost of the rail link to Leiston was

An Aldeburgh branch train hauled by locomotive 65459 waits at Saxmundham station, 19th July 1952. Note the movable section of platform which allows road traffic to cross. (John H. Meredith)

estimated at just over £22,000 and, when trains started on 1st June 1859, there were five each way daily with two on Sundays.

The extension of the branch to Aldeburgh (named Aldborough until 1880) was approved in April 1859 and services began on 12th April 12th 1860. The town was provided with an extravagant station for the size of the branch, built in anticipation of the traffic to come. With the railway available, fishing greatly increased and, in the following years, as many as 70 tons of sprats and other fish were sometimes despatched by rail in one day.

On 1st August 1862, the East Suffolk line and its branches were incorporated into the Great Eastern Railway (GER) which did much to encourage traffic with cheap rates and excursions. Even so, by 1868, Aldeburgh passenger services were reduced to four each way daily and there were none on Sundays. From 1906 there were occasional through coaches which ran daily to and from Liverpool Street. On rarer occasions, visits were made by the 'Eastern Belle' touring train hauled by a GER Claud Hamilton 4-4-0.

J15 0-6-0 no 65459 ready to haul a passenger train from Aldeburgh to Saxmundham 19th July 1952. The branch survived for passengers until September 1966. (John H. Meredith)

A quiet day at Aldeburgh station in 1952. Despite earlier optimism by the railway authorities, Aldeburgh had failed to develop as a major resort. (John H. Meredith)

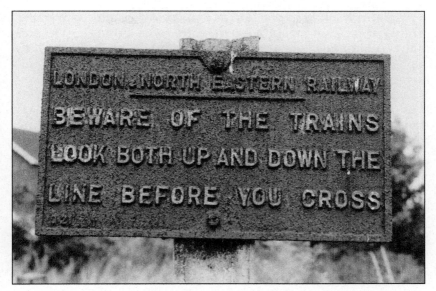

This LNER warning notice can still be found not far from the former Leiston station. Leiston closed in September 1966 but the Aldeburgh branch between Saxmundham and Sizewell remained open for atomic traffic. (Author)

In an attempt to boost traffic, the GER opened a halt at Thorpeness where a garden centre and country club had been developed. Old railway carriage bodies comprised the booking office and waiting room but the halt was too remote from any centre. It was also considered that Aldeburgh station was badly sited to encourage day trippers, so traffic suffered. Despite this, the LNER (after grouping in 1923) continued through trains and excursions until September 1939 when war broke out.

During hostilities, an emergency timetable was introduced and through trains from Aldeburgh to London were withdrawn. Beaches were wired off and holiday visitors no longer came. Evacuees came to the area from London but they were soon to move on again when invasion seemed a possibility. From 1940, armoured trains toured the line, each carrying a six-pounder gun from the first tanks used in the First World War. These lasted until 1943 by which time the Allies were gaining the offensive and Leiston station was handling airfield traffic.

Aldeburgh failed to develop as a major resort and with traffic limited it was soon apparent the line was doomed. Despite many economies, passenger traffic came to an end on 12th September 1966 but a line between Saxmundham and Sizewell power station remained open for atomic traffic.

Today there is little along the old branch to recall the past. At Leiston the old platform edge can be found and over the years two old cast-iron LNER notices have warned 'Beware of the trains . . .' The railway cottage near Thorpeness is an attractive private property surrounded by a golf course. Possibly players over recent years looking for lost balls have been surprised to find the remains of Thorpeness halt platform in the undergrowth!

11
A Branch Line To Southwold

Halesworth to Southwold

Before the Southwold Railway came into existence in 1879, passengers reached Southwold by horse-drawn omnibus from Darsham station on the East Suffolk line which was about nine miles away. (Lens of Sutton)

In October 1875 public meetings took place in Southwold to press for a railway. The small fishing village and trading port at the mouth of the river Blyth was increasing in popularity as a 'watering place' and wanted a standard-gauge link with the East Suffolk line. At the meetings, however, the locals were persuaded that a low cost narrow-gauge railway would meet their needs. A Southwold Railway Bill was presented to Parliament and agreed on 24th July 1876.

After delays caused by landowners, work on a line of nearly nine miles began on 3rd May 1878. Being a single-track 3 foot gauge line it was lightly engineered, although a swing bridge was necessary at Southwold across the river Blyth. When services began on 24th September 1879, a luncheon was held at

117

A train enters Southwold station c1910. Southwold Railway opened on 24th September 1879. It was a single-track 3 foot gauge line with initially four daily trains for the nine mile journey. (Lens of Sutton)

the Swan Hotel, Southwold. During the speeches, the contractor, Mr Chambers, regretted the delays and pointed out his disappointment over the apathy in the town to get the railway going. Certain people, he said, had done a great deal to cause problems and no good had come of it.

Trains between Halesworth and Southwold were initially four daily each way and the time taken for the journey was 37 minutes. There were three intermediate stations at Wenhaston, Blythburgh and Walberswick although the latter two were opened subsequently in December 1879 and during 1882 respectively. The Board of Trade had determined that the maximum speed along the line was 16 miles per hour. This was rigidly adhered to and Rule 92 in the company's regulations stated, 'No train shall be run at a greater speed than 16 miles per hour and the engine driver is liable to two years' imprisonment if convicted of so doing'!

Coaches were six-wheeled with open-ended balconies and lit by oil lamps. In the booklet *Memories of the Southwold Railway*, A. Barrett Jenkins wrote about a schoolgirl who apparently once

118

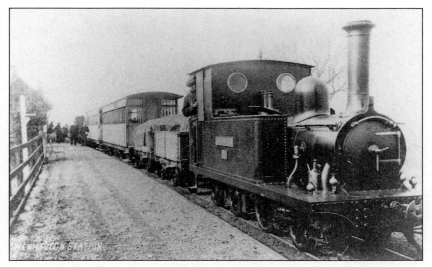

2-4-2T Southwold, no 1, built 1893, prepares to haul a mixed load from Wenhaston station, one of the three intermediate stations on the line. Leaving Wenhaston towards Southwold the train continued close to the river Blyth. (Lens of Sutton)

lost her ticket and, since the lights were not very bright, she turned up the lamp wick to find it. This caused the lamp's glass to smoke up and the guard who collected the tickets did not notice the out-of-date ticket offered to him!

Inside a coach the appearance was much like a tramcar. The seats were of wood, installed along the sides of the coach and covered with a strip of carpet. The carriages were considered airy and spacious and a local paper, *The Halesworth Times*, wrote, 'We trust they will do much to revolutionise our present stupid and, to unprotected females and sometimes males, dangerous system of railway travel . . .'

The Southwold Railway initially possessed three small blue 2-4-0 locomotives which had been purchased from Sharp Stewart of Manchester. Within four years, finances became sufficiently difficult that one had to be returned to the manufacturers, with the remaining two, *Halesworth* and *Blyth*, being re-purchased and leased back to the railway. The first locomotive was converted to 3 foot 6 inches gauge and subsequently sold to the

119

2-4-0T Blyth no 3, originally built in 1879, leaves Southwold for Halesworth. The line closed in 1929 although the railway was not finally demolished until 1941 during the Second World War when any scrap iron was requisitioned under emergency powers. (Lens of Sutton)

Santa Maria Railway in Columbia. By 1893, matters had improved and a 2-4-2T was purchased to become no 1 and called *Southwold*.

Despite the fact that space had been allowed for doubling the track at some future date, this was never done. The line remained single throughout except for a passing loop at Blythburgh. In 1907 the swing bridge at Southwold was renewed at considerable cost. This included widening and strengthening the line to allow conversion to standard gauge at some future date, should the GER or, later, the LNER take the line over. In 1902 a Railway Order authorised an extension to Kessingland to meet a GER branch from Lowestoft and agreed conversion of the gauge. When an offer to purchase the line came from the LNER in 1923, the Southwold Railway turned it down!

Throughout its life passenger traffic remained light but there were occasional busy times. On August Bank Holiday 1899 alone, 415 return tickets were sold and 33 single tickets. By 1913 the number of passengers carried per year had increased to

Southwold station around 1910. Today the site is used by the Suffolk and Ipswich Fire Authority and in addition a police station and police houses occupy the area. (Lens of Sutton)

108,677 and a dividend on ordinary shares was possible at two per cent. By the following year a branch had been constructed to Southwold harbour but it came too late, for the First World War had countered all prospects of fishing. Also in 1914 a new locomotive, a more powerful 0-6-2T named *Wenhaston* was purchased.

After the war there was continued satisfactory traffic but costs were rising, leaving no room for renewals or expansion. In 1922 a further two per cent dividend was paid but this was to be the last. The beginning of the end came in April 1928. Southwold Corporation allowed motor coaches to operate within its boundaries with the result that the railway lost the majority of its passenger traffic. Rail fares were dropped from 2s 3d to 1s 6d for the return journey with cheaper rates during the holiday season but the competition was too great.

At a meeting of the railway company, the chairman reported that with bus competition the Southwold Railway could not go on without help from the Corporation or the LNER. This was unlikely from the Corporation who had brought about the problem and the LNER were now not interested in taking over

The last remaining span of the old swing bridge across the river Blyth was finally removed in 1977 to make way for a footbridge. The original bridge supports are still in use. (Author)

an ailing company. Closure was fixed for 11th April 1929 with the last train due to leave Southwold at 5.25 pm and return at 7.02 pm.

A local paper of 12th April 1929 described the events on the day:

'Tragedy and comedy were mixed when scores of people gathered at Halesworth to see the Southwold Railway closed down after a life of fifty years.

When the frail train started its last journey its four carriages were jammed with 150 people. As the train steamed out, the little booking office was besieged by people asking for tickets as souvenirs.

The train had gone only ten yards when a woman grabbed her small son's hat and started to collect money for the engine-driver. Everyone showered silver into the hat.

On arrival at Southwold a wreath was placed on the

Thanks largely to the efforts of the Halesworth Railway District Circle, a redundant signal box from Halesworth has been reconstructed in the grounds of Halesworth Middle School complete with accessories and a signal. (Author)

smokebox of the engine. People did not know whether to laugh or cry, for the closing down of this railway had caused a great deal of distress. The employees, numbering thirty, received notice of its closing down only two weeks ago.'

The railway was finally demolished during the Second World War, in 1941. Rolling stock was destroyed and oxy-acetylene cutters assisted in the cutting up of the locomotives. Any scrap iron had been requisitioned under the wartime emergency powers. The main structure of the swing bridge had been destroyed earlier in the war during the threat of invasion. Sale of the scrap material realised around £1,500 which was held on deposit.

By the early 1960s the demands of road traffic required a bridge over the A12 to be dismantled and another bridge near Halesworth was part demolished. At about the same time, a liquidator was appointed to wind up the affairs of the company and distribute any monies available to those entitled. In 1963 Southwold station site was compulsorily acquired for use by the Suffolk and Ipswich Fire Authority who required the area for a fire station. When a new police station and police houses were added in 1968 on the remainder of the yard, the old booking office finally disappeared. In 1977 the last remaining span of the old swing bridge together with the temporary Bailey bridge of 1947 were removed so that a new footbridge could be built on the original railway bridge supports.

At Halesworth there is no sign of the narrow-gauge line station adjacent to the standard-gauge track of the East Suffolk line, although bridge abutments can be seen on the nearby B1123. At Halesworth Middle School, one of the Halesworth station's signal boxes complete with all its accessories plus a signal have been preserved in the school grounds. This large-scale reconstruction was very much thanks to the efforts of the Halesworth Railway District Circle which helped to make the scheme possible.

The Southwold Railway failed largely through the company's own follies. Had earlier offers of purchase been accepted, or had the harbour branch not been delayed until 1914, then it just might be there today. But it seems that salvation could still be possible. In August 2005 'The Journal' in Southwold published an article indicating that plans exist to rebuild the old railway. The scheme, estimated to cost £6.5 million, is spearheaded by the Southwold Railway Society which claims that the line will avoid sensitive hen reed beds and the need for a level crossing at Mights Bridge Road to reach a station at the seafront. The society points out that the scheme has considerable local support and, subject to the availability of finance and to planning application to be submitted before the end of 2005, trains could be running again within a minimum of three years.

Such a plan to reduce traffic on already crowded roads and with a link to the main line at Halesworth can surely only be of great benefit to the local townsfolk..

12
Lines Around Bishop's Stortford

Audley End to Bartlow
Bishop's Stortford to Braintree
Elsenham to Thaxted

Lifting track at Saffron Walden just after closure of the line to passengers in September 1964 and to goods in December 1964. Notice of closure had caused many protests from the townsfolk, some of whom had marched with banners reading, 'Don't saw off our branch'! (Lens of Sutton)

Audley End to Bartlow

The Essex market town of Saffron Walden acquired its name from the saffron crocus, the cultivation of which was an important industry from the reign of Edward III until towards

Ashdon Halt on the single-track line from Audley End to Bartlow complete with an old GER coach as waiting room. (Lens of Sutton)

the end of the 18th century. Saffron, still the symbol of the town, was used as a dye, a medicine and a condiment. However, the townspeople had realised by the mid-19th century that the main railway lines had passed them by and endeavours were made to put the town on the railway map.

The ECR had refused to build a branch so initiative was taken by the local Gibson family, wealthy Quaker bankers, who helped to finance the Saffron Walden Railway. The company was incorporated in 1861 but it was not until four years later, on 21st November 1865, that trains reached the town from Audley End on the main Bishop's Stortford to Cambridge line. Within another year, the line was extended to Bartlow giving the Saffron Walden Railway access to the Cambridge to Colchester route.

The company kept going but only with difficulty. Gibson's Bank gave frequent loans but in the end the company sought help through an Official Receiver. On 1st January 1877, the GER purchased the line outright for £70,750 in stock and continued to run it merely as a country branch. Thanks to the railway, Saffron Walden survived as a market with a malting and a cement works introduced in the 1870s. Until 1894 a through train to London was run, otherwise services comprised some six daily over the whole route plus a further dozen between Saffron Walden and the main line at Audley End.

By the 1950s popularity of the branch had dropped dramatically with passengers turning to road traffic. Push and pull services were introduced for economy, these giving way later to diesel railbuses. When an inquiry was held to consider the line's closure there was a storm of protest from the townsfolk. At a resumed inquiry held at the end of 1963, demonstrators held banners reading, 'Don't saw off our branch'. Yet despite objections, and serious concern at the reliability of a proposed replacement bus service, the last train left Saffron Walden at 8.09 pm on a Sunday night in September 1964. Amid the noise of a railbus siren and detonators placed on the track, the train made its way back to the Cambridge depot.

In the *Walden Weekly News* in 1949, somebody signed 'C. M.' wrote:

'If you ever come to Walden by the single railway track,
You're advised to place your luggage firmly on the rack,
And walk the two odd miles at a steady, easy pace,
For it will prove the quickest way of getting to the place.
There have been tales, perhaps untrue, of our own local train,
When, all the travellers getting in and getting out again,
Still found themselves at Audley End – the driver very kind,
Had brought the engine home – and left the carriages behind!'

Bishop's Stortford to Braintree

According to an ancient custom of the manor of Dunmow in Essex, said to have been instituted in 1244, a flitch of bacon is given to any married couple who, after a year of marriage, can swear they have maintained perfect harmony and fidelity during that time. The practice was revived in 1855 and in 1857, during celebrations, the Eastern Counties Railway offered day

A general view of Bishop's Stortford station taken from the south on 23rd February 1952. On the left an 0-6-2T LNER class N7/3 no 69713. (John H. Meredith)

return tickets for the price of a single fare to the nearest stations at either Bishop's Stortford or Braintree with 'conveyances' to take visitors on to Dunmow.

It was to be another twelve years before Dunmow got its own station, an intermediate stop on a line from Braintree to Bishop's Stortford. Trains had reached Braintree from Witham, on the main Colchester line, in 1848 and the extension through Dunmow to Bishop's Stortford followed on 22nd February 1869. Yet the Bishop's Stortford, Dunmow & Braintree Railway had got into financial difficulties even before it had opened. It was saved from ruin by the GER which absorbed the company in 1865.

The take-over gave the GER a useful link between the Cambridge main line and the Essex coast resorts. Even so, the line was hardly used for such a purpose except for occasional excursions from Bishop's Stortford to the coast. Much of the time the line served passengers to Braintree only, while freight traffic comprised coal, sugar beet and general goods. On 7th

Dunmow station on the Bishop's Stortford-Braintree branch. In earlier times there were excursions to the town which had an ancient custom whereby a flitch of bacon was given to any married couple who, after a year of marriage, could prove perfect harmony. (Lens of Sutton)

Felsted station (spelt Felstead until 1950) on the Bishop's Stortford-Braintree line just before closure to passengers in March 1952. A two coach passenger set is hauled by a 2-4-2T LNER (ex-GER) class F5 no 67196. (John H. Meredith)

129

A turntable at Braintree photographed on 8th September 1955. Goods traffic to Bishop's Stortford lasted until 1969 whereas the Braintree-Witham branch has survived to the present time with electrification in 1979. (John H. Meredith)

November 1910, a halt was opened at Hockerill, less than a mile by road from Bishop's Stortford station. Few people used the halt but it did prove useful in one respect since it was well placed for the 19th hole of the town's golf course!

In 1922, the GER, still seeking to develop traffic, opened two further halts along the line. These were at Bannister Green (just over four miles from Braintree) and at Stane Street (near the area known locally as Takeley Street). Since the halts were very small, notices were placed in the coaches warning passengers not to alight until the guard had lowered a set of steps.

The line survived until 3rd March 1952 for passengers (except for occasional excursions), yet goods traffic lingered until final closure in 1969. By comparison, the Braintree-Witham section has fared well. Electrified in 1979, a mixture of through or part trains to and from Liverpool Street and local workings to and from Witham provide a useful service.

Elsenham to Thaxted

On 31st March 1913, the Elsenham and Thaxted Light Railway was officially opened by Sir Walter Gilbey and a special train hauled by two Jubilee class R24 0-6-0 tank locomotives and carrying GER officials and press representatives left Elsenham for Thaxted at 1.25 pm. After speeches, the official party returned by train where lunch was served. It was probably the only time that a restaurant car was seen along the Thaxted branch.

Much of the inspiration behind the line had come from Sir Walter Gilbey of Elsenham. Apart from being a prominent landowner, he was also the founder of the well known firm of wine merchants, W. and A. Gilbey. The branch acquired the nickname 'The Gin and Toffee line', partly from the Gilbey family and partly through the confectionery manufacturers, Lee's of Thaxted.

It was a most unusual railway. There was a speed restriction of 25 mph, there were never any signals and level-crossings

An 0-6-0T LNER class J67/2 no 68609 ready to leave with a passenger set from Thaxted on 23rd August 1952. The branch, known as 'the Gin and Toffee line', closed to passengers on 13th September 1952. (John H. Meredith)

131

were ungated. Throughout much of its life elderly six-wheeled coaches were used and shunting at the intermediate station of Sibleys was carried out by tow rope. There was a goods loop at the station and the locomotive manoeuvred wagons from the other track! There were also three halts along the line although passengers were usually few in number.

The line prospered for the first ten years of its existence and, after 'grouping' in January 1923, it became part of the LNER. During the Second World War the number of trains was drastically cut but, by the time full services were returned in 1948, many passengers had forsaken the railways. Replacement of the uncomfortable six-wheeled coaches with modern bogied vehicles did little to bring people back.

In April 1951, British Railways announced plans to close the line although it was over a year before this was to take effect. On 13th September 1952, the final down train left Elsenham hauled by J69/1 class locomotive no 68579. The three ex-GER corridor coaches, decorated for the occasion with streamers, carried over 400 passengers and in the guard's van there was a black-draped coffin bearing the inscription 'Died Waiting'.

The Elsenham to Thaxted branch had the distinction of being one of the last to be constructed and one of the first to close.

13
Branch Lines To The
Essex Coast

Witham to Maldon
Woodham Ferrers to Maldon
Wivenhoe to Brightlingsea
Kelvedon to Tollesbury Pier

Maldon East station c1905. The branch closed completely in 1966 yet this unexpectedly grand building survived to become The Great Eastern Motel. (Lens of Sutton)

Witham to Maldon

It seems strange that the section of the original Maldon, Witham & Braintree Railway from Witham to Braintree should have survived today to prosper with electrification, yet the line from

Witham to the ancient port of Maldon closed to passengers in September 1964. The company had a difficult start in life. Authorised in 1846, the ECR shrewdly agreed it could cross its main line, thus in effect creating two branches requiring reversal at Witham. Subsequently in the same year, after suggesting to the local directors that the line might not pay, it took over the small company after falsely promising high dividends.

The Witham to Maldon line, opened to passengers on 2nd October 1848, was built very economically with timber used where possible instead of bricks. Yet in contrast, Maldon East station was built extravagantly in the style of a Jacobean mansion with ornate chimneys and Dutch gables and, across the front, a nine-arch arcade.

There is a story, quite unproven, that the station's splendour is due to the fact that the deputy chairman of the ECR, David Waddington, was an election candidate at the time it was built. It seems that quite a number of men, most of them freemen of Maldon and thus entitled to vote, were offered employment on railway construction some time before the election. In order to keep the potential voters occupied, the station was made bigger and more elaborate than it need have been! The workers, who were dismissed shortly after the poll, were paid a guinea for their efforts and they gained the nickname of 'guinea pigs'.

Daily services from Witham to Maldon varied from seven to nine. The branch encouraged market gardening and locally-grown peas became a speciality. Fruit growing also prospered with Wickham Bishops, an intermediate station, becoming a despatch point. Yet the line was not to survive. Closure to passengers came on 7th September 1964 with goods traffic following on 18th April 1966 after which time the track was ripped up.

Woodham Ferrers to Maldon

First trains from London to Southend were promoted by the London, Tilbury & Southend Railway (LT&S), reaching there in 1856. The GER's need for independent access to the resort was not met until October 1889, when a branch was opened from its

Woodham Ferrers, seen here in GER days, is today an intermediary station on the single track line which provides electric services between Wickford and Southminster. A line from Woodham Ferrers to Maldon, known as the New Essex line, opened in 1889 to survive for passengers only until 1939. (Lens of Sutton)

main Colchester line at Shenfield. Passenger trains reached Wickford on 1st January 1889 and Southend Victoria on 1st October of the same year.

With its alternative route to Southend being established, the GER became anxious to open up remote parts of southern Essex by promoting several new ventures. These routes became known as the 'New Essex' lines and one of these was a branch from Wickford via Woodham Ferrers to Southminster. This opened to passengers on 1st July 1889, and three months later, on the same day GER trains reached Southend, a further branch opened from Woodham Ferrers to Maldon West with an intermediate station at Cold Norton. Beyond tracks went on to link with either the line to Witham or to the 1848 Maldon station. Maldon was renamed Maldon East on 1st October 1889 and became 'Maldon East and Heybridge' on 1st October 1907.

135

Southminster station, c1910, in GER days. Today the station is a terminus on the line from Wickford with a weekday service providing some 20 electric trains each way daily including a number of through Liverpool Street workings. (Lens of Sutton)

Cold Norton station c1910 on the Woodham Ferrers-Maldon line. Despite the hopes of the railway authorities, commuters did not settle in this bleak part of Essex. (Lens of Sutton)

Passengers pose at Maldon West station c1905. The branch from Woodham Ferrers opened on 1st October 1889, the same day that GER trains first reached Southend from Shenfield. (Lens of Sutton)

Passenger traffic generally was poor and few London commuters were anxious to move to this bleak part of the county. By 1914 the number of daily trains had dropped to five and from mid-1916 to mid-1919 the line was closed as a wartime economy measure. During the 1920s two halts were opened to encourage traffic. Yet despite economies the line finally closed to passengers just after the outset of the Second World War, on 10th September 1939. Goods traffic survived until the 1950s.

Wivenhoe to Brightlingsea

When the devastating East Coast floods came on 31st January 1953, many thought that the opportunity would be taken to close down the branch from Wivenhoe to Brightlingsea. Three miles of the line had been washed away yet, following pleas to

A single-track branch from Wivenhoe to Brightlingsea opened in 1866 to survive until June 1964. An LNER (ex-GER) class J15 0-6-0 locomotive no 65432 waits at Brightlingsea on 28th December 1948. (John H. Meredith)

protect the interests of Brightlingsea and the important oyster trade, train services were resumed by the following December.

Initially the Wivenhoe & Brightlingsea Railway (W&B) was unable to raise sufficient capital, and only when the GER offered one-third of the cost was the project able to go ahead. The branch, single track and with no intermediate stations, opened on 18th April 1866. It was five and a half miles in length with its route following the north bank of the river Colne to cross Alresford Creek by a swing bridge before entering the Brightlingsea terminus. In June 1893 the GER purchased the line outright.

The original Brightlingsea station with its overall roof had a very draughty reputation, with the North Sea's winds circulating around the structure during much of the year. Little wonder the townsfolk were delighted when it burned down on New Year's Eve, 1901! It was replaced by a simpler station which had the advantage of being adjacent to a fish loading dock at the end of the line. Passenger traffic improved with

Colchester station c1910 on what is today's London to Norwich Intercity line. Until 1964 some eight trains ran each way daily from Colchester to Brightlingsea. (Lens of Sutton)

many day trippers arriving to enjoy the local amusements and occasional boat trips.

Despite much publicised special cheap-day tickets and excursions to London, the W&B suffered the usual competition from the roads and the line eventually closed on 15th June 1964. Brightlingsea station has gone but much of the trackbed along the bank of the river Colne can still be found, serving as a defence against flooding.

Kelvedon to Tollesbury Pier

The Kelvedon, Tiptree & Tollesbury Pier Light Railway (K&T) was authorised by the Board of Trade on 29th January 1901 when a Light Railway Order was granted. The intention of the line was to help local farmers during a period of depression, serve the local fruit growers and also assist the Wilkin's jam factory. A. C. Wilkin was one of the instigators of the scheme

The 1,770 foot Tollesbury Pier, photographed in January 1949, was built in May 1907. The pier track was lifted in 1940 shortly before the pier was breached as an anti-invasion measure. (John H. Meredith)

with the firm donating land for what became Tiptree station.

Services from Kelvedon to Tollesbury began on 1st October 1904 without any formal ceremonies. The GER, after some hesitation, worked the line, almost nine miles long and of standard gauge. There was a speed restriction of 16 mph along the lightly built route, reduced to 10 mph 200 yards before any level crossings. When a J67 0-6-0T locomotive was employed during the early years, it was converted to a 2-4-0T by removing the forward coupling rods, hopefully to reduce wear on the many sharp curves to be encountered.

Another purpose of the line was to assist revival of the ailing and isolated Tollesbury Pier. The line was extended to the pier on 15th May 1907 but little activity developed. The section closed after only 14 years' use, on 17th July 1921, although during the Second World War the stretch usefully accommodated four WD locomotives with mobile guns. In 1940 the pier's track was removed and the pier isolated from the shore as an anti-invasion measure.

Initially, carriages on the K&T had been four or six-wheeled stock, third class only and equipped with retractable steps since a number of platforms were almost at rail level. When the Wisbech & Upwell tramway closed in 1928, the branch acquired six further coaches. Two further coaches became available when the Stoke Ferry branch closed in September 1930. After refitting at Stratford works, they reached the K&T in 1931 enabling some earlier coaches, now 54 years old, to be withdrawn.

The line to Tollesbury closed to passengers with effect from 7th May 1951 although goods traffic continued for a number of years, mainly serving a fruit collection centre just beyond Tiptree. When the last train left Kelvedon on Saturday, 5th May 1951, it collected some 430 passengers in the three coaches during the journey. On the engine's smokebox was chalked, 'Born 1904 . . . Died 1951', and on the bunker was the warning, 'There may be many a poor soul have to walk'.

14
More Lost Causes

Cambridge to Mildenhall
A Branch Line to Hadleigh
Diss to Scole
Mellis & Eye Railway

Steam at Cambridge in June 1951. On the left, LNER 4-4-0 locomotive class D16/2 no 62543 and, on the right, class D16/3 no 62531, a later development of the same class. (John H. Meredith)

Cambridge to Mildenhall

The GER line from Cambridge to Mildenhall was opened from Cambridge to Fordham on 2nd June 1884 with the final stretch to Mildenhall completed the following year on 1st April. The branch was built to help ailing local agriculture and generally develop the sparse and thinly populated area; yet through most of its life it ran at a loss.

The line survived for passengers until 1962 yet efforts to

142

GER Cambridge station before motor transport took over. By the early 1920s three trains ran each way between Colchester and Mildenhall via Fordham on weekdays only. (Lens of Sutton)

economise had existed throughout. Towards the end of the 19th century, the GER had used some of its obsolete locomotives and rolling stock on the branch but this had not always proved a saving when it came to fuel or repairs. In 1913, push-pull trains were introduced thus eliminating the locomotive turn-round at Mildenhall, but these gave problems on busy market days when it was necessary to cope with additional passengers and extra luggage. Eventually the GER went back to standard trains using a conductor guard and, once again, using older coaches.

During the economies of the 1950s, British Railways introduced a number of 54-seat, four-wheel railbuses which for a time brought new life to the branch. Yet even such increased efficiency did not stop the Mildenhall branch becoming an early victim to the Beeching cuts. Passenger traffic stopped on 18th June 1962 with goods traffic following within three years.

Much of the trackbed today has been ploughed over, yet a number of bridges still exist. Among the stations that have

LNER locomotive no 2783 at Mildenhall awaits departure to Cambridge on 8th June 1951. Mildenhall closed to passenger traffic in 1962 to become a private residence retaining many of the station features. (John H. Meredith)

'Claud Hamilton' class 4-4-0 no 1858 awaits departure from platform 1 at Cambridge probably hauling a Liverpool Street stopping train. Built in Stratford in 1904 it lasted until scrapping in 1955. (Lens of Sutton)

144

Great Northern Railway locomotive no 50 Class D1 receives a final polish before departing from Cambridge. This super-heated 4-4-0, built in June 1909, was the last of its class. It became LNER no 2201 and was withdrawn in July 1947. (Lens of Sutton)

survived is Mildenhall, currently a strictly private residence. The property has been tastefully converted and the surrounding land developed into a spacious garden. The platform still exists and the old platform building carries many recollections of the past. Even the old booking office window has been blended into the present decor. Truly an idyllic setting for any rail enthusiast!

A Branch Line to Hadleigh

Hadleigh, in Suffolk, once a centre of the East Anglian cloth trade, first saw passenger trains on 2nd September 1847 when the Eastern Union & Hadleigh Junction Railway opened a seven and a quarter mile branch line from Bentley. The line was basically an Eastern Union Railway (EUR) venture to block ECR progress towards Norwich and, at the same time, provide a possible through route, via Lavenham, to the Midlands. The

A branch line from Bentley to Hadleigh opened in 1847. The Eastern Union Railway hoped to build on via Lavenham to the Midlands and also block ECR progress towards Norwich. Despite such endeavours, Hadleigh remained a terminus. (Lens of Sutton)

EUR took over the small company in 1848 although the furthest the branch reached was Hadleigh. The track was single but provision was made for double track plus a spur facing Ipswich in case the line ever reached further.

Some two weeks after the line opened there was an unfortunate mishap. Despite the fact the station was still incomplete, an excursion had been arranged to take trippers to an annual regatta at Ipswich. Whilst a hundred or so people were waiting on the platform, a strong gale sprang up causing the newly-completed wall along the back of the platform, 14 feet high and 40 feet long, to collapse upon them. Nobody was killed but many were seriously injured.

Throughout the line's life passenger traffic was light. For much of the time there were five trains each way daily and three on Sundays. Goods traffic benefited for a time while Hadleigh's milling and malting prospered. Further local industry included coconut matting, clothing and the manufacture of machinery.

As time passed, the town's population fell and the isolation of

Hadleigh station building photographed after closure to passengers in 1932.
When visited in 1998 it was being renovated to become a private residence.
(Author)

the area from a main railway line discouraged growth. With buses established between Hadleigh and Ipswich by the early 1930s, the end for passenger traffic became inevitable. Closure came on 29th February 1932 although goods traffic survived until April 1965 with Hadleigh continuing as a useful agricultural railhead.

When visited in October 1998, Hadleigh station building was still there. It was being renovated to become a private residence.

Diss to Scole

Not far from Alan Bloom's Steam Museum at Bressingham once existed another prominent market gardener whose foresight led to a prosperous business. When the Eastern Union Railway arrived at Diss in 1849, wealthy landowner, William Betts, saw an opportunity to get his produce speedily to the expanding London markets. By 1850 seven miles of standard-gauge track

147

Diss station on the main Ipswich to Norwich line. Between 1850 and 1886 a seven-mile privately-owned railway operated between Diss and Scole serving a market gardening estate. (Author)

linked the Frenze Estate at Scole with the main line at a junction just north of the present Diss station. Since this was a railway on a private estate no Act was needed.

At Scole the branch line served Frenze Hall, two large brickfields and a barn. Two locomotives did the work, one a small 0-6-0 tank and the other a smaller 0-4-0 tank. There were no signalling problems since only one was used at a time. The locomotives filled with water from a tank which was replenished by pumps powered by traction engines. Betts had 15 wagons and, when these were insufficient, he hired further wagons from the ECR.

For many years Frenze Estate flourished. There were even times when a passenger service became available for the workers and a few local folk by using improvised wagons with planks for seats! However, when Betts died in 1885, all activity came to an end. The line was closed and taken up the following year.

Mellis & Eye Railway

When in 1849 the main line to Norwich passed several miles to the west of Eye, the town's population decreased as a result. An Act, promoted by local interests, followed in 1865 authorising a branch with a capital of £20,000. However, the Mellis & Eye Railway did little to reverse the trend. The three mile long branch opened after many delays on 2nd April 1867 when a locomotive hauled eight four-wheeled coaches along the line. The local inhabitants turned out to watch the event but there were few celebrations.

The railway continued its quiet existence and freight carried consisted mainly of coal and beetroot. In 1898 the company was incorporated into the GER and in 1922, in the hope of improving passenger traffic, a halt was opened close to the bridge at Yaxley. Matters hardly improved and on 2nd February 1931, the branch closed to passenger traffic. Freight services survived until July 1964.

All that remains of Eye station is the station-master's house, today used as an office. The station buildings have been demolished and the site is in industrial use. (Author)

A station survived at the junction of Mellis, on the main Haughley to Norwich line, until 7th November 1966. The platforms and the tall brick 'Mellis Junction' signal box were removed when electrification came to the Norwich line. And, much to the relief of local residents, the level-crossing gate became automatic.

Standing today on what was once a road bridge over the railway at Yaxley (just off the A140), it is possible to look across the fields and determine where the railway track led to Eye. The bridge was once known as 'The Duke's Bridge' for it had been hoped that the then Duke of Edinburgh might be available to open the line when services began in 1867, though this did not prove possible. At the terminus, Eye, the platform and station buildings have gone. Only the station master's house remains.

When the line closed in 1931, *The Suffolk Chronicle & Mercury* gave details of the Eastern Counties buses that would take over, and observed that, as far as the railway was concerned, the town was being 'Eye-solated'!

Conclusion

The decline of many of East Anglia's lines began in the 1920s. Buses were providing a more flexible service than the trains and road haulage was on the increase. An early casualty was the narrow-gauge Southwold Railway from Halesworth to Southwold which closed on 12th April 1929. Other branches soon followed; 1930 saw the closure to passengers of the Stoke Ferry branch and the Mellis & Eye Railway.

More lines followed, yet during the Second World War many found new uses supplying the numerous East Anglian airfields with petrol or bombs. After the war losses increased and in 1959 much of the M&GN system closed altogether. In March 1963 proposals were made in a report which became popularly known as the 'Beeching Plan'. Basically, the idea was to keep lines considered suitable to rail traffic and give up the remainder. It was claimed that one third of the rail system in Britain carried only 1% of the total traffic!

The resultant closure of lines over the next decade became almost a landslide throughout the region. Rail traffic fell dramatically with passengers and freight becoming almost completely reliant on road transport. Today the basic main lines of the past survive but the lives of the few remaining branches must surely be on a short term basis.

The Norfolkman and *The Broadsman* may have gone, yet the diesels that took over from steam are themselves slowly disappearing. Electric services reached Norwich from Liverpool Street in May 1987. Despite such advances, there are many places where steam trains are not forgotten at the numerous preserved lines or steam museums throughout the area.

Yet what of the future for East Anglia's railways? Rail privatisation, we were told, would give us an exciting future.

Now press reports tell us that 'complaints about late, cancelled and overcrowded trains have soared since the start of rail privatisation. Figures point to an alarming deterioration in services'. The Channel Tunnel, although providing rapid links with European capitals, still has to provide high-speed trains in the UK and the tunnel still has to prove itself financially.

During research in the region, the author was appalled at the very high density of traffic on East Anglia's roads, private and commercial. What plans are in hand to avoid total congestion of our highways within just a few years while railway lines remain inadequately used? There is talk, but only talk, of 'piggyback trucks' by rail, a feature popular in many European countries. Container traffic could also certainly be maximised. And what is the future for rural train services which surely remain particularly vulnerable to closure, these alone absorbing a large portion of the railway's annual subsidy?

A brighter aspect of the future is the possibility that trains might return to redundant lines. During 1998 there were renewed efforts to re-open the Cambridge-St Ives-Huntingdon railway which would, it was claimed, 'relieve pressure on the busy A14'. There was talk of re-establishing the railway line from Witham to Maldon. Such ideas must one day come about to relieve our choked roads. There have been discussions to revitalise more of our inner cities. The successes of the Docklands Light Railway, the Tyne and Wear Metro and many others have brought about a flood of applications to build new systems elsewhere. Croydon introduced trams during 1999. Further towns have been considered – including Norwich. Currently, consideration is being given to the possibility of a light rail link between the city centre and Norwich airport which is on the northern edge of the city.

Back to the past again, part of an article in the *East Anglian Daily Times* of 1st June 1971 on vanishing branch lines read:

'For some people, the rural scene has never been quite the same since the branch railway lines closed. The little local trains chuntering fussily through the quiet countryside under billowing plumes of steam were an accepted part of rural life that is still sadly missed by many old enough to remember them.'

152

Opening and Final Closure Dates of 'Lost' Lines to Regular Passenger Traffic

Line		Opened	Final Closure
King's Lynn to Dereham		1846/1848	1968
Wymondham to Dereham	*1	1847	1969
Bentley to Hadleigh		1847	1932
Magdalen Road to Wisbech		1848	1968
Witham to Maldon		1848	1964
Dereham to Fakenham		1849	1964
Sudbury to Shelford		1849/1865	1967
Diss to Scole		1850	1886
Yarmouth (South Town) to Beccles		1854/1859	1959
Tivetshall to Beccles		1855/1863	1953
Wells to Fakenham	*2	1857	1964
Wickham Market to Framlingham		1859	1952
A Branch to Snape (goods only)		1859	1960
Saxmundham to Aldeburgh		1859	1966
Chappel & Wakes Colne to Haverhill	*3 *4	1860/1863	1962
King's Lynn to Hunstanton		1862	1969
Spalding/Sutton Bridge/South Lynn		1862/1865	1959
Audley End to Bartlow		1865/1866	1964
Long Melford to Bury St Edmunds		1865	1961

Heacham to Wells		1866	1952
Sutton Bridge/Wisbech/			
Peterborough		1866	1959
Wivenhoe to Brightlingsea		1866	1964
Mellis & Eye Railway		1867	1931
Thetford to Swaffham		1869/1875	1964
Bishop's Stortford to Braintree		1869	1952
Thetford to Bury St Edmunds		1876	1953
Melton Constable/			
North Walsham/			
Yarmouth Beach		1877/1883	1959
King's Lynn/Fakenham/			
Melton Constable		1879/1882	1959
Halesworth to Southwold		1879	1929
Forncett to Wymondham		1881	1939
Melton Constable to Norwich		1882	1959
Denver to Stoke Ferry		1882	1930
Wroxham to County School	*5	1882	1952
Wisbech-Upwell Tramway		1883/1884	1928
Melton Constable to Sheringham	*6	1884/1887	1964
Cambridge to Mildenhall		1884/1885	1962
Woodham Ferrers to Maldon		1889	1939
North Walsham to Cromer		1898	1964
Yarmouth to Lowestoft		1903	1970
Yarmouth Beach to Gorleston		1903	1953
Kelvedon to Tollesbury Pier	*7	1904	1951
Haughley to Laxfield	*8	1908	1952
Elsenham to Thaxted		1913	1952

*1 Wymondham to Dereham owned by Mid-Norfolk Railway Preservation Trust

*2 Wells to Walsingham now the Wells & Walsingham Light Railway

*3 Chappel & Wakes Colne station is the site for the East Anglian Railway Museum

*4 Stretch near Sible & Castle Hedingham station now Colne Valley Railway

*5 Wroxham to Aylsham now the Bure Valley Railway

*6 Holt to Sheringham now the North Norfolk Railway
*7 Tollesbury to Tollesbury Pier – opened 1907, closed 1921
*8 The former Brockford & Wetheringsett station site is now the
    Mid-Suffolk Light Railway Museum

Bibliography

In compiling *Lost Railways of East Anglia*, I have referred to numerous sources which include the following and which can be recommended for further reading:

Allen, Cecil J. *The Great Eastern Railway* (Ian Allan Ltd)

Body, Geoffrey *Railways of the Eastern Region Volume 1: Southern Operating Area* (Book Club Associates by arrangement with Patrick Stephens Ltd)

Comfort, N. A. *The Mid-Suffolk Light Railway* (Oakwood Press)

Cooper, John M. *The East Suffolk Railway* (Oakwood Press)

Course, Edwin *Railways Then and Now* (B. T. Batsford Ltd)

Gordon, D. I. *A Regional History of the Railways of Great Britain, Volume 5, The Eastern Counties* (David & Charles)

Jenkins, A. Barrett *Memories of the Southwold Railway* (L. & S. Rexon, Southwold)

Joby, R. S. *Forgotten Railways – East Anglia* (David & Charles)

Moffat, Hugh *East Anglia's First Railways* (Terence Dalton)

Paye, P. *The Ely & St Ives Railway* (Oakwood Press)

Perry, Gordon and Park, Michael *A Visitor's Guide to the North Norfolk Railway* (North Norfolk Railway, Sheringham)

Philbrick, Keith *Wells & Walsingham Light Railway* (The Wells & Walsingham Light Railway)

Quayle, H. I. and Jenkins, Stanley C. *Branch Lines into the Eighties* (David & Charles)

Rhodes, John *The Midland & Great Northern Joint Railway* (Ian Allan Ltd)

Stapleton, N. J. *The Kelvedon and Tollesbury Light Railway* (Forge Books and Stour Valley Railway Preservation Society)

Wallis, A. T. *Colne Valley Railway Guide and Stock Book Limited* (Colne Valley Railway Preservation Society)

Walsh, B. D. J. *The Stour Valley Railway* (Connor & Butler on behalf of the East Anglian Railway Museum)

Wright, C. M. *The East Anglian Railway Museum* (Stour Valley Railway Preservation Society)

Young, Michael *Colne Valley Album* (Apex Publications, Cambridge)

INDEX

Printed in Great Britain
by Amazon

75877546R00092